Who Do You Think You Are?

a guide to understanding the new man

Douglas W. Graves

Published by
Word of Faith Center
1350 S. Rainier
Kennewick, WA 99337

CONTENTS

ACKNOWLEDGMENTS

One very important truth that I have learned over the years is that you never achieve anything significant without the input of others. Networking is the only way to win in life. The same is true with this book. Without the hard work of certain people, this book may not have been a reality.

I first would like to thank my best friend, my mentor, and my constant strength, the Holy Spirit. It is because of His faithfulness to reveal truth that this book is even in existence. I want to thank my former secretary of seventeen years, Louise Brady, for the hours and hours of editing, compiling, design work . . . the list goes on. All of the effort and dedication she has given on her own time has made this book a reality. Thank you to my present secretary, Lynae Carter, for helping refine the second printing and for all of her special insights in design and layout.

Writing "Who Do You Think You Are" truly has been a team effort. I believe that all the input will pay off as we see how God speaks to each reader and assists them in becoming all they can be in Christ.

INTRODUCTION

The human race has always faced a major challenge: discovering what and who they are. Everyone wants to have a sense of purpose in life. It is an identity issue. Many Christians have not yet discovered who they are. They suffer from negative and destructive mindsets as a result of an abusive past. Some have adopted worldly and unbiblical concepts of themselves without realizing it. Others have allowed their church's personal beliefs and traditions to mold them into a person that is not of God's mold. God's picture of us must be realized if we, as members of the human race, are going to rise up and fulfill the destiny that He has for our lives. God can only do through us what we allow Him to do. If we do not see ourselves as God sees us, it will sabotage God's destiny for our lives. Man cannot know himself without clear definition from the creator.

God is waiting for us to wake up to the fact that He has created us anew in the person of Christ. God has provided a new identity for you as a believer. It is part of your inheritance as a child of

God. Only until you believe it, receive it, and act on it will you begin to experience it. The only way of knowing who you are in Christ is through the revelation of God's Word.

You are not who the devil says you are. You are not who people say you are. You are not even who you think you are because you can deceive yourself. James 1:22 says, "But be ye doers of the word, and not hearers only, deceiving your own selves." You are who God says you are. It is not up to the created to tell the Creator what he will be. Romans 9:20 says, "Nay but, O man, who art thou that repliest against God? Shall the thing formed say to him that formed it, Why hast thou made me thus?" Church, rise up! What God has made you in Christ must become a reality in you. As you allow the Word of God to develop your inner man with the revelation of who you are in Christ, you will have solved the identity crisis for yourself. As you rise up in who you are in Christ you will rise above defeat, sin consciousness, disease, poverty, inferiority and weakness, and you will begin to soar on the wings of eagles.

CHAPTER 1

TRUE IDENTITY

OPENING OUR EYES

Have you ever had anyone say to you, "Who do you think you are?" What they were really asking was, "Why do you live the way you do? Why do you have the attitude you have? Why are you being the way you are?" I want to use this same phrase to challenge your thinking. What is making your life tick? Who do you think you are?

The Body of Christ needs a clear understanding from God's Word regarding who they are in Christ. Your life will begin to radically change when you get a revelation of your true identity from God's point of view. I have seen born again children of God live miserable, bound-up lives because they never allowed their minds to be renewed to the truth of what they had truly become in Christ. As Christians, they continued to see themselves the same way they saw themselves before they became children of God.

> *The Body of Christ needs a clear understanding from God's Word regarding who they are in Christ.*

A Christian mind that has not been renewed to the truth of his new identity in Christ will be robbed of the abundant life that God has provided for him. God wants you to have a deeper understanding of what He has made you in Christ. With this understanding comes great blessings to your life.

> "That the God of our Lord Jesus Christ, the Father of glory, may give unto you the spirit of wisdom and revelation in the knowledge of him:
>
> The eyes of your understanding being enlightened; that ye may know what is the hope of his calling, and what the riches of the glory of his inheritance in the saints,
>
> And what is the exceeding greatness of his power to us-ward who believe, according to the working of his mighty power,
>
> Which he wrought in Christ, when he raised him from the dead, and set him at his own right hand in the heavenly places."
>
> — Ephesians 1:17-20

In my 22 years of pastoral ministry, without question the number one problem that people struggle with is their personal identity. The false concepts that people have of themselves have been destroying their self-worth, their destiny, their families, splitting churches, and dividing races. God wants to enlarge your understanding so that you can get free from the false concepts that oppress, suppress, and depress your true self-image.

> "Dear, dear Corinthians, I can't tell you how much I long for you to enter this wide-open, spacious life. We didn't fence you in. The smallness you feel comes from within you. Your lives aren't small, but you're living them in a small way. I'm speaking as plainly as I can and with great affection. Open up your lives. Live openly and expansively!"
>
> — *II Corinthians 6:11-13, The Message*

How you see yourself definitely determines how your life will be lived out. Someone said, "You cannot consistently live in a way that is inconsistent with the way you see yourself." You can only live the God kind of life when true identity in Christ is rediscovered. It's time to open our eyes and step into what God has prepared for those that love Him.

> "But as it is written, Eye hath not seen, nor ear heard, neither have entered into the heart of man, the things which God hath prepared for them that love

him...Now we have received, not the spirit of the world, but the spirit which is of God; that we might know the things that are freely given to us of God."

— *I Corinthians 2:9,12*

WHOSE MOLD ARE YOU IN?

"Don't let the world around you squeeze you into its own mould, but let God re-mould your minds from within, so that you may prove in practice that the Plan of God for you is good, meets all His demands and moves towards the goal of true maturity."

— *Romans 12:2, Phillips*

This scripture clearly reveals to us what should and should not mold our lives. God intended for His Word to develop our true identity. We are instructed to be transformed — undergo radical metamorphosis — by the renewing of our minds. What you derive your identity from determines whether or not you will find true significance and experience God's good, acceptable, and perfect will for your life. The concepts, beliefs, and philosophies of life that we identify ourselves with mold our lives and determine how we will live.

Goodspeed translates I Corinthians 15:47-49 in a very understandable way:

> "The first man is of the dust of the earth; the second man is from heaven. Those who are of the earth are like him who was of the earth, and those who are of heaven are like him who is from heaven, and as we have been like the man of the earth, let us also try to be like the man from heaven."
>
> *— I Corinthians 15:47-49, Goodspeed*

The two Adams represent a picture of humanity and describe two types of human existence. You are either in the first Adam or you are in Christ, the last Adam. Your true identity as a human being will be derived from identification with one of these two regardless of race or social status. Everybody lives out one of these two existences.

*W*hat you derive your identity from determines whether or not you will find true significance and experience God's good, acceptable, and perfect will for your life.

The first Adam represents the family of man fallen and separated from God. This family was produced through his transgression. Adam, our head and representative, separated the human race spiritually from God through his disobedience and birthed a humanity joined to their new father, the devil.

"In this the children of God are manifest, and the children of the devil."

— I John 3:10(a)

The disobedience of the first Adam produced a fallen humanity — Satan gained an offspring. The disobedience of the first Adam produced a humanity earmarked by self-will, independence, and rebellion. Their thought processes became earthly, sensual, and devilish. The fall of Adam produced a humanity with a totally different mentality and way of life, one that put mankind in a mold far below the spiritual condition and mentality of God's original creation. The fall of Adam produced a race of degenerates. That word might sound offensive to some, but the word "degenerate" simply means to lose the qualities proper to race or kind. You see, when the first Adam fell, mankind lost its true identity, and when true significance was lost, the instinctive search for significance began. Humanists search for significance apart from their creator. This road is a dead end and can never bring true significance since only God can reveal to man his true identity. Only the Creator can truly define and explain the creation. Darwinism promotes that mankind is a freak accident with no real purpose. To expect the soul to find significance from that is futile. People's search for identity has led them into gangs, false religions based on performance, and social groups. One may feel a common bond in these groups, but

Jesus Christ is the perfect picture of who we really are.

true identity cannot be found in joining a club or organization. Identity is only found in the person of the Lord Jesus Christ, the new head and representative of the new creation. Jesus Christ is the perfect picture of who we really are.

> **"There is neither Jew nor Greek, there is neither bond nor free, there is neither male nor female: for ye are all one in Christ Jesus."**
>
> **– *Galatians 3:28***

So let's consider the last Adam — the Lord Jesus Christ. Jesus, the last Adam, is God's provision for man to rediscover true identity and be delivered from the false concepts we have as a result of the first Adam's fall. Jesus is the head and representative of a new race of beings. The Bible describes Jesus as the last Adam. God has appointed Him to be the new head and representative of a new humanity. Jesus, the last Adam, through supernatural conception by the Holy Spirit, was born into this life sinless. During His walk on this earth, He lived a life of complete obedience. Jesus willingly allowed Himself to be crucified for the first Adam's disobedience, go to hell for all of us, and be raised up on the third day. His willingness to submit to God's will and live a life of total obedience and sacrifice legally reconnected mankind back to God in a brand new spiritual relationship. Jesus, God's appointed head, has brought into reality a new humanity, one totally free from sin, Satan, spiritual death and disease and reconnected to God in a new relationship, canceling out the result of the first Adam's choice to disobey. The first Adam's disobedience corrupted God's original creation. Jesus' life of obedience has reconnected and recreated a fallen race of corrupted humanity. (Romans 5:15-19)

When we allow the truth about Jesus to renew our minds, we will begin to experience a powerful inner transformation. A whole new way of seeing ourselves will begin to emerge and an incredible new-creation life will start to demonstrate itself through our personal behavior. We will begin to see for ourselves the wonderful new identity that God has given us as those in Christ.

"Therefore if any man be in Christ, he is a new creature: old things are passed

away; behold, all things are become
new."

— II Corinthians 5:17

You and I, in Christ, have each become a "new
creation" of being. Do you know what that means?
Do you understand how new creations think, act,
and live? You need to, because in Christ it's who
you now are. Through Christ, God has brought into
existence a whole new creation.

The Bible says you are a God kind!

**"Behold, what manner of love the
Father hath bestowed upon us, that we
should be called the sons of God."**

— I John 3:1(a)

**"For ye are all the children of God by
faith in Christ Jesus.**

**For as many of you as have been bap-
tized into Christ have put on Christ."**

— Galatians 3:26-27

God's work in Christ has given humanity an
incredible opportunity to receive a brand new
spiritual nature through the revelation of God's
Word. We can now put off the mentality and false
identity inherited through the fall of the first
Adam. The fallen condition of the human race, and
its corrupted mentality, is so far below what God

created us to really be in the original creation. The fall of Adam has produced a human race with a false and corrupted belief about who and what we really are as humans. It is time for all of us to discover our true identity revealed through the work of Christ, God's new representative.

> **"That ye put off concerning the former conversation the old man, which is corrupt according to the deceitful lusts:**
>
> **And be renewed in the spirit of your mind;**
>
> **And that ye put on the new man, which after God is created in righteousness and true holiness."**
>
> *— Ephesians 4:22-24*

We are instructed to put off the way of the old, be renewed in our minds, and put on what we truly are now in Christ. Thank God, He did not leave us blinded to His true and original plan for mankind but has made a way for us to regain relationship with Him and take on our true identity. This isn't just a salvation message — it's a wake-up call to be all that God has designed your life to be. I hear people say, "Well, you know, we're only human." But this is what keeps people in carnality. Carnality is fleshly, worldly, Adamic thinking.

In I Corinthians 3:1-3 Paul says, that the reason

the Christians were carnal and living wrong was because they thought like mere humans think.

> "And as for myself, brethren, I found it impossible to speak to you as spiritual men. It had to be as to worldlings — mere babes in Christ.
>
> I fed you with milk and not with solid food, since for this you were not yet strong enough. And even now you are not strong enough: you are still unspiritual.
>
> For so long as jealousy and strife continue among you, can it be denied that you are unspiritual and are living and acting like mere men of the world?"
>
> — *I Corinthians 3:1-3, Weymouth*

You and I, now in Christ, have become God's very own offspring, not mere men of the world. Being a child of God isn't just a theological or intellectual statement - it's a statement of reality. In Christ we are not to identify with the worldly man in Adam, but the new man in Christ. We are truly a product of a new creation because of Christ. God has changed what we were spiritually and has become our Daddy God. We are not what we used to be in Adam. Jesus didn't just die to take away our sins. He was crucified, buried, and rose again to undo the condition brought about by the first Adam's fall and bring into existence, through His resurrection, a new family of man. It's time we began to think, talk, and act as if the Word of the Gospel were true. To not accept the new truth about our new selves is to let Jesus' death, burial, and resurrection be in vain. In Christ, we have now been freed from a corrupted, perverted image into a new image created in God's image and likeness. As believers, we must let go of the old and be renewed in our minds to the new mentality in Christ. Greatness and freedom await our souls as we embrace the truth through our minds' renewal.

CHAPTER 2

MIXED MESSAGES

THE STATE OF THE UNRENEWED MIND

A simple observation of human behavior reveals that something is missing in the way we truly see ourselves. God's creation is plagued by inferiority, insecurity, low self-esteem, pride, jealousy, envy, and a multitude of other mental baggage. This was not what God originally created humanity to be. We must realize that because of the fall of Adam there are many concepts that dominate our minds, seeking to dictate to us a false identity message. Instead of building lives on spiritual truth, some have built their lives around Adamic, natural information. That has sent mixed messages into our souls. It's like in the Peanuts comic strip when Lucy walks up to Charlie Brown, who's hard at work on a birdhouse. "How are you doing, Charlie Brown?" she asks. "I'm a lousy carpenter," he replies. "I can't nail straight, I'm always splitting the wood, I'm nervous, I lack confidence, I'm stupid, I have poor taste and no sense of design, but all those things considered, I'm all right." We laugh at this because it hits a little closer to home than we'd like to admit. Many believers, instead of receiving God's truth for their lives, have accepted concepts that are destructive and counterproductive to God's destiny for their lives.

God doesn't want you living with mixed messages. The devil loves it because as long as you stay in that mixed-up state of mind you will never soar with eagles — you will peck with the chickens. Please don't misunderstand me. I am an extremely optimistic person. My desire is to stir you up to truly examine yourself and ask, "What really makes me behave the way I do? What or who has been programming my mental computer? Am I living, thinking, and talking in a way consistent with new-creation truth?" To find the answers, you must examine yourself in the mirror of God's Word.

> *Am I living, thinking, and talking in a way consistent with new creation truth?*

> **"For if any be a hearer of the word, and not a doer, he is like unto a man beholding his natural face in a glass:**
>
> **For he beholdeth himself, and goeth his way, and straightway forgetteth what manner of man he was."**
>
> **— James 1:23-24**

When we look long enough into the mirror of

God's Word, our new identity will become crystal clear - if we take the Word at face value.

>**"But we all, with open face beholding as in a glass the glory of the Lord, are changed into the same image from glory to glory, even as by the Spirit of the Lord."**
>
>*— II Corinthians 3:18*

Stop living blindly by programmed mindsets that do not reflect who you are in Christ. We all need a clear idea of who we really are. We are created in the image of God. Anything else is far below what we truly have been created to be in Christ. The Word of God is the instrument of truth, revealing how things are now for us from the Creator's point of view.

It's like the story of the ugly duckling. A little swan got separated from his original family and found a place in a family of ducks. He grew up thinking he was a duck, and everyone thought he was ugly. But one day that ugly duckling grew up and began to realize who he really was. He was not ugly at all; he was beautiful.

> *Stop living blindly by programmed mindsets that do not reflect who you are in Christ.*

It's time we see ourselves that way. God does! This is what freedom is really all about. When we stop allowing something other than God's truth to define our true identity, we will experience true freedom. When we allow our minds to agree with the Word of God, the corruption and deception due to Adam's fall is removed from our mentality. The result is an incredible sense of well-being and inner-peace.

THE DIABOLICAL PLAN

Destroying true identity in the human race is the major objective of the enemy. His works have produced a race of powerless, defeated, diseased, inferior beings. The human race is plagued with fear, depression, and insecurity. From the time you were born Satan has sought to destroy your self-worth and blind you from God's true identity in Christ. Abuse, whether sexual, physical or mental, as well as feelings of failure, rejection, addiction and other deceptions are the avenues the enemy uses to tear down the dignity and rightful place that God designed for the human race. Let's look at

From the time you were born, Satan has sought to destroy your self-worth and blind you from God's true identity in Christ.

the Word and find out why the devil has targeted this area of humanity so strongly.

> **"And God said, Let us make man in our image, after our likeness: and let them have dominion over the fish of the sea, and over the fowl of the air, and over the cattle, and over all the earth, and over every creeping thing that creepeth upon the earth.**
>
> **So God created man in his own image, in the image of God created he him; male and female created he them."**
>
> **— *Genesis 1:26-27***

God's desire was to create a being in His class. Some think that God created man because He was lonely. Creation had no selfish motivation. God is a giver. His desire was to create a being in His class capable of experiencing the kind of life that He Himself experiences, a being capable of true intimacy and fellowship. God wasn't talking to the angels when He said, "Let us" make man. God the Father was talking to the other members of the Godhead — God the Son and God the Holy Spirit. I believe that angels were present, including Lucifer, and were aware of what God was about to do in His creation of man. This is extremely important to understand so that you might grasp the reason for Satan's intense hatred toward God and the human race. I believe Lucifer was outraged that God would make a being closer to Himself than he was. Lucifer was the over-covering cherub in heaven. The Bible says there was found within him musical ability. Many believe he led the worship of heaven.

> "Thou hast been in Eden the garden of God; every precious stone was thy covering, the sardius, topaz, and the diamond, the beryl, the onyx, and the jasper, the sapphire, the emerald, and the carbuncle, and gold: the workmanship of thy tabrets and of thy pipes was prepared in thee in the day that thou wast created."
>
> — *Ezekiel 28:13*

What an awesome place to be. He was most likely the closest created being to God until God made man in His own image and likeness. Angels are different types of beings than man. I talked to a woman who thought that when people died they would become angels and grow wings. No, we are not angels nor will we ever be angels. We possess, as the creation of God, an estate with God that no other beings have. I don't believe that God loves us more than angels,

We possess, as the creation of God, an estate with God that no other beings have.

but I do believe it's a different type of love. I John 3:1 reveals that there is a certain manner of love that God has bestowed on His creation, those created in His image and in His likeness.

> **"Behold, what manner of love the Father hath bestowed upon us, that we should be called the sons of God."**
> — *I John 3:1(a)*

We were created as an exact duplication of His kind. We were created as much like God as possible without being God. No, this is not a cult doctrine. You are not God and you are not going to have your own planet to eventually populate with another human race. But the fact is that God's creation of man bears His godly characteristics. False religions and New Age doctrine seek to twist and pervert the real truth of our identity in God, our Creator. New Age and humanism seek to define the human with God out of the picture. The truth is, without God, any attempt to know yourself is a waste of time. God is the only one who can complete man and define a true picture of mankind. Man, without a relationship with God through Jesus Christ, is lost.

But the fact is that God's creation of man bears His godly characteristics.

Outside of this relationship he cannot find true identity and significance as a person. Only God can define it. This identity comes only from God, our true source of identity. It can only be realized when we are brought back into union with our Creator and allow the Word to renew our minds to truth. Lucifer's fall from heaven was connected to his extreme jealousy of man. He hates the fact that God has a race bearing His image and likeness.

> "How art thou fallen from heaven, O Lucifer, son of the morning! How art thou cut down to the ground, which didst weaken the nations!
>
> For thou hast said in thine heart, I will ascend into heaven, I will exalt my throne above the stars of God: I will sit also upon the mount of the congregation, in the sides of the north:
>
> — *Isaiah 14:12-13*

The main issue of his arrogance centered around things that God exclusively reserved for mankind. Psalm 8:5 says that man was created a little lower than angels.

> "For thou hast made him a little lower than the angels, and hast crowned him with glory and honor."
>
> — *Psalm 8:5*

The Hebrew word used for "angels," however, is Elohim, a word describing God. The translators had a hard time with this one. But, in fact, we were created a little lower than God. This was a place higher than angels, and Lucifer was jealous of it. He wanted to sit in a prominent place. The believer was created to sit with Jesus at God's right hand, a place of prominence.

> **"And hath raised us up together, and made us sit together in heavenly places in Christ Jesus."**
> — *Ephesians 2:6*

Psalm 8:6 reveals that God's creation was created to sit in a place of authority over all the works of God's hands.

> **"Thou madest him to have dominion over the works of thy hands; thou hast put all things under his feet."**
> — *Psalm 8:6*

Lucifer never had this authority and was jealous of it. Later you will see how Lucifer successfully robbed Adam of his ability to have dominion. In Isaiah 14 Lucifer let the cat out of the bag.

> **"I will ascend above the heights of the clouds; I will be like the most High.**
>
> **Yet thou shalt be brought down to hell,**

to the sides of the pit."

— *Isaiah 14:14-15*

Lucifer blurted out the very thing that was really eating at him — to be like the most High, to have that which was solely reserved for the family of man. This is the very thing that corrupted Lucifer. In his pride and beauty he was not satisfied with what God had made him to be, but arrogantly demanded from God what God had reserved for the human race.

> "Thou art the anointed cherub that covereth; and I have set thee so: thou wast upon the holy mountain of God; thou hast walked up and down in the midst of the stones of fire.
>
> Thou wast perfect in thy ways from the day that thou wast created, till iniquity was found in thee.
>
> Thine heart was lifted up because of thy beauty, thou hast corrupted thy wisdom by reason of thy brightness..."

— *Ezekiel 28:14-15,17(a)*

After Lucifer's fall his name became Satan, the archenemy of both God and the family of man. Satan's plan, fueled by hate and jealousy, moved him to organize an army of rebellious spirits to defame and destroy the identity of the human race in hope that it would be lost forever. His objective is to destroy the image of God in man so that man never discovers it or enjoys it. Satan figures if he can't have it, nobody will. His objective is to see to it that man never takes his place as God's off-spring. Let's look at the main tools the devil uses to destroy the image of God in man.

SIN

In the beginning, when God created man, Satan was already on the scene with a plan to destroy. His diabolical goal was to destroy the God-likeness that man bore from being created in the image and like-ness of God. Notice the enemies focus on mankind's God-likeness.

> "And the serpent said unto the woman, Ye shall not surely die:
>
> For God doth know that in the day ye eat thereof, then your eyes shall be opened, and ye shall be as gods, know-ing good and evil."
> — *Genesis 3:4-5*

What a farce! The devil knew that man had been created in God's image and likeness. That is what the human race was like before the fall. And it's what God restored to us in Christ. But some people are so afraid to accept the truth about their identity that the enemy actually talks them out of it. Jesus said, "Ye are gods."

> "Jesus answered them, Is it not written in your law, I said, Ye are gods?

> If he called them gods, unto whom the word of God came, and the scripture cannot be broken..."

> *— John 10:34-35*

Now you aren't a "god" like Father God, but you are gods in the sense that you are His created offspring. We, as new creations, are either sons of God, or we are not. Let's accept the truth. Look hard at God's original plan for man before the fall. You will see that human beings were a perfect duplication of God, our Creator. Refusing to accept your identity as established by God is to allow the enemy to thwart God's destiny for your life. Remember, you cannot live in a way that is inconsistent with the way you see yourself. Satan immediately moved in on Adam

Refusing to accept your identity as established by God is to allow the enemy to thwart God's destiny for your life.

and Eve to entice them into disobedience because he knew man's spirit would then be cut off from the source of life and his true identity.

Sin is a killer of identity. Sin is designed to destroy the human personality. The definition of sin is to miss the mark, to come short of the glory of God.

> **"For all have sinned, and come short of the glory of God."**
> — *Romans 3:23*

In Exodus 33:18-23; 34:5-6, Moses was allowed to see God's glory. It was a reflection of God's very own nature and character. This glory is what man was originally created to reflect in his life. In Christ, the very glory of God is restored to man.

> **"To whom God would make known what is the riches of the glory of this mystery among the Gentiles; which is Christ in you, the hope of glory:"**
> — *Colossians 1:27*

God's glory is for man to once again receive right standing and right relationship with Him, thus becoming a partaker of God's divine nature. (II Peter 1:4) This has always been His plan for man. Sin is Satan's tool to destroy one's personal identity. Sin derails man's ability to really live in harmony with the image and likeness of his Creator. Sin blinds men from receiving the truth about their significance and worth as human beings. The devil knew exactly what he was doing. He knew exactly what would happen when Adam and Eve ate of the forbidden fruit. Romans 5:17 reveals the tragedy of the fall of the human race in Adam.

> **"For if by one man's offence death reigned by one; much more they which receive abundance of grace and of the gift of righteousness shall reign in life by one, Jesus Christ."**
>
> *— Romans 5:17*

The Weymouth translation says, "Death made use of the one individual to seize the sovereignty." Through Adam's transgression, death, the nature of Satan, robbed man of his ability to reign in life. Adam's disobedience changed the spiritual condition of all humanity. The fall transferred authority over to the devil, where Satan then began his evil and oppressive reign over the human race. From the time of the fall of Adam until Jesus, man has been under the lordship of spiritual death; the wicked nature of man's new father ruled with tyranny and vengeance over the human race. Our enemy has oppressed, killed, diseased, and impoverished mankind. He has influenced men blinded from the truth who have murdered, raped, and robbed fellow human beings. Satan has turned man against man to fulfill his evil plan to destroy. Men and women with lost identity live lives with no definite purpose or destiny.

> "Who is a wise man and endued with knowledge among you? Let him shew out of a good conversation his works with meekness of wisdom.
>
> But if ye have bitter envying and strife in your hearts, glory not, and lie not against the truth.
>
> This wisdom descendeth not from above, but is earthly, sensual, devilish."
>
> *— James 3:13-15*

The human race has been duped by the enemy but has been unconscious of it.

> "In whom the god of this world hath blinded the minds of them which believe not, lest the light of the glorious gospel of Christ, who is the image of God, should shine unto them."
>
> *— II Corinthians 4:4*

Jesus, in His earthly walk, painted a picture for all to see, of what it's really like to live the way God truly intended. Man apart from God has no way of understanding true identity. His mind is darkened by selfishness, pride, cultural influences, negative family upbringing or religious indoctrination, and until the truth of God's real design is known, man will stay bound by these false concepts.

> "This I say therefore, and testify in the Lord, that ye henceforth walk not as other Gentiles walk, in the vanity of their mind,
>
> Having the understanding darkened, being alienated from the life of God through the ignorance that is in them, because of the blindness of their heart:
>
> Who being past feeling have given themselves over unto lasciviousness, to work all uncleanness with greediness.
>
> But ye have not so learned Christ;
>
> If so be that ye have heard him, and have been taught by him, as the truth is in Jesus:
>
> That ye put off concerning the former conversation the old man, which is corrupt according to the deceitful lusts;
>
> And be renewed in the spirit of your mind;
>
> And that ye put on the new man, which

after God is created in righteousness
and true holiness."
– *Ephesians 4:17-24*

God's Word has been given to us so that we
might know who we now have been created to be in
the Last Adam, The Lord Jesus Christ. When this
becomes a reality in us, and we allow the good
news of Christ to change the way we think, we will
never be the same.

When we accept Christ's work personally, and
as we confess Him as our
new Lord, God's Spirit erad-
icates the nature of death
from our spirit and recreates
us as children of God with a
new spiritual nature. When
God puts His Sprit of life in
your spirit, death is annihi-
lated and you become a new
species of being. Once you
have been born again and
made alive spiritually, you become a candidate for
mind renewal.

> *Jesus, in His
> earthly walk,
> painted a picture
> for all to see,
> of what it's really
> like to live the
> way God truly
> intended.*

Mind renewal is where you really begin to experience the new life in Christ. Your thinking, emotions, choices, and self-worth are transformed into
what God gave your spirit in the new birth. If you

are a Christian living in sin, repent so God can stop the corruptive power of sin. Sin means "to miss the mark." The enemy uses sin to drive you into condemnation, guilt, and inferiority so that you will not experience self-worth, victory, and boldness. Sin is counter-productive to experiencing the reality of a new identity. Forsake sin at all costs.

As we realize what Christ has done for us and put on this new-creation mentality, Satan's ability to kill, steal, and destroy will be over. Once you and I realize the blessing of this new life in Christ, we will forsake sin and its evil plan to separate us from experiencing the truth in our inner man. We must rise up and reclaim our rightful place as God's creation. We must rid our lives of the things that destroy godly identity, and we must allow the Word of God to renew our minds so we may be like our Creator.

> **"And have put on the new man, which is renewed in knowledge after the image of him that created him."**
> — *Colossians 3:10*

Notice again that your identity should be identical to the image of your Creator. To be a human and not have a Biblical view of true identity is an accident waiting to happen. It's only as you know the truth that the truth will make you free. When

Adam sinned God called out to him.

"And the Lord God called unto Adam, and said unto him, Where art thou?"

— *Genesis 3:9*

Now God knew Adam's physical location, but He looked down and saw his lost, fearful, spiritually dead, insecure human being and said, "Where are you? Where is the person I created you to be? Where is the creature that bears my image and likeness? He is gone." And it remained that way until Christ came to earth to undo what Adam transferred to the human race. This is what God is saying to the Church today: "Where is the new creation? Where are you, child of God?" Does God see in us fear, inferiority, insecurity, pride, and jealousy, or does He see His image and likeness in the earth through His people? Sin causes men and women to put on fig leaves instead of being clothed with the image and likeness of God. If we continue to hold fast to our inferiority, sin, guilt, and condemnation, we allow the enemy to win over our lives. When we accept the truth, the enemy's works are destroyed and you experience the freedom of God's plan for your life.

> W*e must rise up and reclaim our rightful place as God's creation.*

Someone described the fig leaf as follows:

F - ear

I - nferiority

G - uilt

L - oneliness

E - xile

A - nger

F - rustration

FEAR manifests itself in hiding from God and others for fear of being hurt. The root of fear is rejection. Fear destroys confidence and enslaves the human soul. It causes people to shrink back from the challenges of life. Fear motivates a person to accept defeat before the battle has even begun. Fear destroys faith.

INFERIORITY is the feeling that our lives are not as good as other people's. We have this over-whelming sense that others have all the looks, skills, abilities, and personality and that we don't have quite as much to offer. It makes us feel small and insignificant when we are around people who we feel "have it all." It causes unjustified resentment toward others because of our own low self-esteem. Inferiority is a suppressor and killer of true identity.

GUILT is despising ourselves for not being what we think we should be. Guilt punishes us for our shortcomings. It is man's way of atoning for his own unrighteousness. The only problem is that guilt has no mercy. Its objective is self-destructive — it's a killer of self-image.

LONELINESS is a result of separation from God and others. Loneliness produces the condition of feeling unloved and abandoned. It carries with it a sense of unworthiness as a result of a loss of personal love and concern from others. Again, this is a destroyer of God's plan for your true identity. God said, "I will never leave you or forsake you."

EXILE is the overwhelming sense of abandonment, the inward feeling of not being wanted. It develops a sense of worthlessness. Satan knew this feeling of exile as a result of his willful disobedience. He sought to put man in the same condition of bondage through sin and disobedience. Exile develops a sense of disconnection from God.

ANGER is the frustration of having no self-worth. It manifests itself when a person's life is out of control and he is unable to fix the problem himself. Only God can solve the identity issue and bring lasting peace.

FRUSTRATION is the inability to cope with an unresolved identity crisis. Men and women are lost without a connection to their Creator. That is why self-help books, religion, and the psychic hotlines won't help you. Man was not created to live apart from the spiritual connection with God. That is where we get our identity. Without Jesus Christ, without a divine union, and without Biblical truth, you have no true identity. Your identity is in the person of God Himself because you were created like Him.

Personal sin — as opposed to universal sin — drives us away from God. As a Christian you don't lose your position with God if you sin, but you do lose your sense of identity, your sense of right-eousness, and your sense of faith to be able to come into the presence of God. You lose that bold-ness of life because sin goes to work and begins to destroy. The Bible says that "the wages of sin is death" (Romans 6:23). What is death? Death is not immediately falling over and dying. Death is a spir-itual thing that progressively invades the human soul. Because of guilt, shame, fear, inferiority and low self-esteem, you don't want to be around any-body because you are afraid somebody is going to know what you've done or know who you are. It's like the parable of the prodigal son. He didn't lose his position with his father, but he was not having a good time away from his father. He was in bondage, living like the pigs. All of his friends were gone. He was lonely, guilty and messed up. If you sin and move away from God, you won't attend church or hang around people because you are afraid they will judge you. You stay isolated from others. And while you stay isolated, the devil is killing you. It's a plan of the enemy to snuff out the identity that God has designed for man. You will need to work your way back up, get some confidence back in you, get the Word of God back in you, and get that junk out of your soul.

NEGATIVE PAST LIFE EXPERIENCES

The second tool the enemy uses to destroy true identity is negative past life experiences – things that happened to you as you were growing up. These play a major part in developing your belief system and personal identity. Everything that has gone on in your life from the day you were born until now has affected you. This corruption that we have been exposed to is a result of Adam's fall and Satan's reign over the human race. They are not a product of God's plan for our lives. If we could view a film of your past, we could witness these past life experiences. Everyone has them. Some of them are very painful to look at but they do not have to be what develops your identity. Remember, true identity comes from God, not your experiences in life. Rape does not have to be what molds your life. Molestation does not have to be the factor that molds your life. Divorce does not have to be what molds your identity. Only God and His view can bring true identity. From the time you were born until now, someone, something, your environment, culture or upbringing have been instrumental in programming your thoughts and behaviors. All of us have programmed belief systems within us that control our lives. As young children, our souls were like sponges soaking up all kinds of concepts and we were not aware of the molding going on in our lives. God wants you to really look at why you do things the way you do and see if it's a product of truth or deception and corruption.

The following diagram shows how the soul (mind, will, and emotions) is programmed and how it develops negative belief systems that are ingrained in us until they are renewed by the Word of God.

BELIEF SYSTEM

The first box, Past Life Experiences, is broken into two categories. The first category (A) is long-term exposure to an environment. This could be family upbringing and exposure of your soul to physical, mental, and even sexual abuse. This is

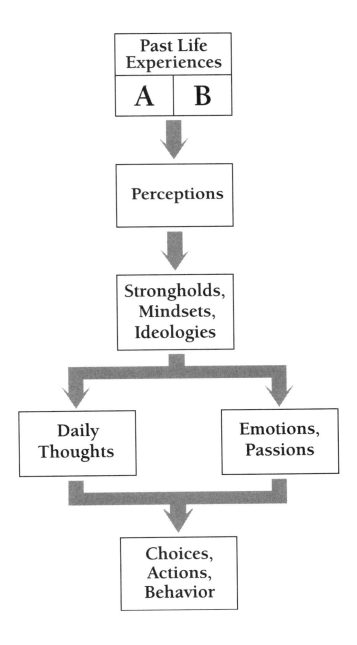

long-term exposure to hurt, rejection, ridicule, and low morals. This exposure to your environment plays a big part in forming how you see yourself. The second category (B) of Box 1 is traumatic experiences, things like rape, incest, divorce, adoption, or a tragic death in the home. These are experiences that leave deep bruises and scars on the self-worth of a human being. These experiences traumatize the soul and leave an incredible impression upon your life. Past life experiences are the springboard for the next step in the process of the development of the human soul.

The second box is Perceptions. This is how your soul begins to assimilate the information coming to you through the experiences you have gone through or are going through. Perceptions are formed through a process found in II Corinthians 10:4-5.

> "For the weapons of our warfare are not carnal, but mighty through God to the pulling down of strong holds;
>
> Casting down imaginations, and every high thing that exalteth itself against the knowledge of God, and bringing into captivity every thought to the obedience of Christ."
>
> — *II Corinthians 10:4-5*

Our thoughts enable us to process information that comes to us as a result of experiences. The thoughts that we contemplate and allow to go on inside our heads determine the next stage in perception, which is knowledge that places itself above or apart from Biblical truth. So our thoughts, whether truth or deception, produce the foundation for our knowledge and education on a subject. The high thing that exalts itself against the knowledge of God develops imagination, the next stage in perception. The Greek work for imagination is "logismos." It is where we derive our English word "Logic." Our thoughts produce our knowledge of a thing as perceived by our own deduction and reasoning. After a process of mental contemplation, the information begins to make sense and we begin to accept it as logic. The danger is that just because we may think it is true and logical, doesn't make it so. Without a reference point for truth, truth and logic can be anything your head wants it to be. In other words, just because your parents divorced when you were young, doesn't mean you are a bad person or you are the reason they divorced. Your experience may play a significant role in your process of developing personal perception of who you are, but the real truth about you, as an individual, is not defined by personal conclusion. Only the Creator can define who you are and enable your mind to arrive at a mental conclusion that is truthful and beneficial to your future. The Word of God is God's source of truth that keeps our mental perceptions founded on truthful logic as defined by our Creator. Anything outside of Biblical truth can and will lead to insecurity, inferiority, fear, unworthiness, and rejection.

Such false perceptions can be on any subject — God, self, sexuality, family, money, church, work, etc. What we perceive as real truth eventually becomes a stronghold or a mindset in our souls, and how experiences in our lives are perceived determines how the strongholds are formed. This brings us to the third box: Strongholds, Mindsets, or Ideologies, which are concepts, opinions and philosophies that have become concrete as absolute fact in your soul. These concrete mindsets are what presently have become the mental foundation for your belief about God, sexuality, money, family and even your personal identity and self-worth. It takes a Holy Ghost jackhammer to break up false mindsets and redevelop your mind in truth. Thank God the Word is designed to pull down destructive strongholds and renew our

> *What we perceive as real truth eventually becomes a stronghold or a mindset in our souls...*

minds with strongholds that come from the Word and bring peace, joy, and a correct self-image. Past life experiences are like a concrete truck backing up to your front door. Perceptions are like the concrete being dumped into your living room. At this early stage the concrete can be removed. But the stronghold is the concrete that has become fully set up. It is an established mindset, a strong, foundational belief that can be true or false.

These first three boxes represent your present belief system. Everybody has some kind of belief system. These boxes represent every human being I've ever met. This is why I tell couples preparing for marriage to realize that they are not marrying a pretty face or good looking body — they are marrying a belief system. Do you really know what it is? This belief system is what you are presently living out. This belief system is also what you are joining yourself to in a marriage union. Most couples never really take the time to really know what they are joining their lives to in a lifetime commitment.

Your belief system, made up of the first three boxes, is a foundation for *the fourth box: Daily Thought Life*. What you think daily about yourself, people, God, sexuality, authority, etc., are all spawned by your programmed belief system.

Your daily thoughts are the major determining

factor of *the fifth box: Passions and Emotions.* I'm aware that some emotions are physiological, but most are a product of thinking based on your mindsets, because of perceptions as a result of past life experiences.

All these previous boxes lead us to *the sixth box: Choices, Action, and Behavior.* Your behavior is a product of the previously mentioned boxes that work in the soul. A couple once brought their child to me and requested that I cast the devil out of him. The child obviously did not want to be there and was quite upset. I had known that the father was an alcoholic and the mother had been involved in several relationships with other men. The parents needed the real deliverance, not the child. The young man just needed love, guidance, and a sense of security. It was sad to watch how the enemy was once again using the situation to destroy the young man's true identity. This is a generational curse. Generational curses that influence the soul of a human being are the transference of three basic elements: spiritual transference, physiological transference, and environmental transference. But the good news is that what is presently in your soul can and will be renewed by God's Word. When this happens, generational curses over our lives are broken.

It is not always an easy process, but it is very profitable to become what God has made you to be.

The only hold the devil has on a child of God is in his or her unrenewed mind. Receiving true identity back into the soul slams the door on the enemy's works against us. It's time to go into battle and reclaim what God has made us to be. People have learned to live by limited and faulty mindsets, and it has allowed the enemy to keep them bound. The strongholds or mindsets that have become concrete in our mentality become the reference library for our daily thoughts and the conclusions we arrive at. For instance, if you have a stronghold of rejection, your daily thoughts will lead you to a logical conclusion that nobody likes you. If you have a stronghold of insecurity, your thoughts will draw the conclusion that you need to perform for people's acceptance. The stronghold will also determine what you are most passionate about in life. If your mindsets are deceived, your passions will be misguided. For instance, if rejection is your mindset, you will be driven to always please people for acceptance. It will be a passion because it is a matter of self-worth. Our thoughts and emotions flip the switch of actions or choices. Our actions create habits and our habits determine destiny.

> *The only hold the devil has on a child of God is in his or her unrenewed mind.*

You can see now why the enemy of your soul does not want you to renew your mind to truth. As long as our souls are corrupted and deceived, our behavior will support the agenda of the enemy: bondage and unfulfilled lives. When we allow the truth of God to renew the spirit of our minds, our behavior will support the agenda our Creator has for us: fruit, freedom, and Godly self-worth. What controls our mind determines our future success or failure. It determines whether God or Satan, truth or deception, will guide your life.

An example of this is found in the book of Exodus. The people of God were in bondage and God sent Moses to deliver them.

> "And I have also heard the groaning of the children of Israel, whom the Egyptians keep in bondage; and I have remembered my covenant.
>
> Wherefore say unto the children of Israel, I am the Lord, and I will bring you out from under the burdens of the Egyptians, and I will rid you out of their bondage, and I will redeem you with a stretched out arm, and with great judgments:
>
> And I will take you to me for a people, and I will be to you a God: and ye shall know that I am the Lord your God,

which bringeth you out from under the burdens of the Egyptians.

And I will bring you in unto the land, concerning the which I did swear to give it to Abraham, to Isaac, and to Jacob; and I will give it you for an heritage: I am the Lord."

— *Exodus 6:5-8*

In this passage, we see God appearing to Moses and revealing to Moses His plan to deliver the children of Israel from bondage. God has heard their cry and remembered the promise He made to Abraham, Isaac, and Jacob to deliver them from bondage and bring them into a place of freedom and abundant life. Their past life experience was scarred by Egyptian slavery and the oppression of Pharaoh. Pharaoh is a type of Satan, and Egypt is a form of the world. God gives us this natural picture to explain what He wants to do in our lives. The Israelites had been put down, rejected, and dominated by a slavery mentality, and they cried out for deliverance. God sent Moses to deliver the people out of bondage, but He took them into the wilderness to get that mentality out of them. He could have taken them right into Canaan land, but He knew if they didn't get rid of that mentality they were not going to go very far. You see, God is not only interested in getting you out of the world, but

He is interested in getting the world out of you. He wants to take the Egypt mentality out of you. He wants to take the control and tyranny of Pharaoh (Satan) and the world out of your soul. When he took them out into the wilderness, He wanted to show the Israelites who He was and who they were as His people. He wanted to demonstrate His power, His mercy, and His love. He wanted to deliver them from a slavery mentality and give them purpose and significance for living. God's desire was to restore their self-worth and dignity, which had been so damaged due to slavery and Egyptian indoctrination.

God brought them into the wilderness to renew their minds, but they never gave up their Egypt mentality. The wilderness was never designed to be a curse. They refused to take the opportunities of that God presented to them through His Word, miracles, and presence. The result was that their minds remained the same, and it eventually became a curse to their future. When the twelve spies were sent to spy out the land, two said they were capable of taking the land, but the other ten said it was hopeless.

> **"And they told him, and said, We came unto the land whither thou sentest us, and surely it flowest with milk and honey; and this is the fruit of it.**

Nevertheless the people be strong that dwell in the land, and the cities are walled, and very great: and moreover we saw the children of Anak there.

The Amalekites dwell in the land of the south: and the Hittites, and the Jebusites, and the Amorites, dwell in the mountains: and the Canaanites dwell by the sea, and by the coast of Jordan.

And Caleb stilled the people before Moses, and said, Let us go up at once, and possess it: for we are well able to overcome it.

But the men that went up with him said, We be not able to go up against the people; for they are stronger than we.

And they brought up an evil report of the land which they had searched unto the children of Israel, saying, The land, through which we have gone to search it, is a land that eateth up the inhabitants thereof; and all the people that we saw in it are men of a great stature.

And there we saw the giants, the sons of Anak, which come of the giants: and we were in our own sight as grasshoppers, and so we were in their sight."

— *Numbers 13:27-33*

The ten spies said they were not able because there were giants in the land, and they were, in their own sight, grasshoppers. They had "grasshopper syndrome." What they were really saying was, "We are just a bunch of nobodies; we don't have the ability." They were holding on to their small, Egypt mentality, not aware that it was sabotaging their future in Canaan. They were allowing their preprogrammed Egypt mentality to determine their destiny. They had been freed physically, but mentally they were still in slavery. One cannot truly be free until his mind is renewed. An Egypt mentality will destroy your destiny. You cannot hold onto the mentality of "not enough" and expect to experience the land of "more than enough."

> "And all the congregation lifted up their voice, and cried; and the people wept that night.
>
> And all the children of Israel murmured against Moses and against Aaron: and the whole congregation said unto them, Would God that we had died in the land of Egypt! Or would God we had died in this wilderness!

And wherefore hath the Lord brought us into this land, to fall by the sword, that our wives and our children should be a prey? Were it not better for us to return into Egypt?

And they said one to another, Let us make a captain, and let us return into Egypt."

— *Numbers 14:1-4*

This is the way a lot of people are today. They are afraid to become what God has called them to be, and they are comfortable staying the way they have always been. Then when somebody rises up and begins to tell them they can be somebody in God, it makes them mad and they seek a captain who will agree with their small thinking. They will build a church around it, or go to a church where that's the way it is taught, so they can feel comfortable and don't have to grow up! Churches like that exist throughout the United States and the world. They teach people what they want to hear. Some people don't want any expectations put upon their lives. They don't want to grow up and be what Jesus called them to be. They don't want to deal with insecurities, rejections and hurts that have programmed their souls. The Israelites sought a captain to take them back to Egypt; they wanted to return to the thing that bound them.

Remember II Corinthians 6:11-13 in the Message translation?

> "Dear, dear Corinthians, I can't tell you how much I long for you to enter this wide-open, spacious life. We didn't fence you in. The smallness you feel comes from within you. Your lives aren't small, but you're living them in a small way. I'm speaking as plainly as I can and with great affection. Open up your lives. Live openly and expansively!"

FAILURES AND DISAPPOINTMENTS

Another tool the enemy uses is previous failure and disappointments in life. Failure and disappointments can be used to frame a mentality of unworthiness. We see this in Judges 6 with Gideon, as he grew up under the oppression of the Midianites.

> "And the children of Israel did evil in the sight of the Lord: and the Lord delivered them into the hand of Midian seven years.

> "And the hand of Midian prevailed against Israel: and because of the Midianites the children of Israel made them the dens which are in the moun-

tains, and caves, and strongholds.

And so it was, when Israel had sown, that the Midianites came up, and the Amalekites, and the children of the east, even they came up against them;

And they encamped against them, and destroyed the increase of the earth, till thou come unto Gaza, and left no sustenance for Israel, neither sheep, nor ox, nor ass.

For they came up with their cattle and their tents, and they came as grasshoppers for multitude; for both they and their camels were without number: and they entered into the land to destroy it."

— *Judges 6:1-5*

Every time the children of Israel had sown for a harvest, the Midianites came and destroyed their increase. They would get so close to breakthrough and then the Midianites would come dash their dreams. Doesn't this sound familiar? These continual disappointments robbed the spirit from the Israelites. Finally they cried out to the Lord.

"And Israel was greatly impoverished because of the Midianites; and the children of Israel cried unto the Lord."

— *Judges 6:6*

So the Lord began to move by raising up a judge. His name was Gideon. And where do we find Gideon? Hiding from the Midianites because he didn't want them to take the little bit that he had. Gideon had the same broken, disappointed mentality in him that the other Israelites had.

> "And there came an angel of the Lord, and sat under an oak which was in Ophrah, that pertained unto Joash the Abiezrite; and his son Gideon threshed wheat by the winepress, to hide it from the Midianites."
>
> *— Judges 6:11*

Gideon was hiding his wheat from the Midianites. The wheat was a small, insignificant amount, but Gideon was protecting it. This is what so many people do. They hoard the little increase they have and stop sowing big. It's a trick of the enemy to keep your harvest in life small. The root is fear and unbelief.

It's a trick of the enemy to keep your harvest in life small. The root is fear and unbelief.

Then God told Gideon that he was being sent to deliver the Midianites and that he really was a mighty man of valor! Gideon began his excuses.

> "And the angel of the Lord appeared

unto him, and said unto him, The Lord is with thee, thou mighty man of valour.

And Gideon said unto him, Oh my Lord, if the Lord be with us, why then is all this befallen us? And where be all his miracles which our fathers told us of, saying, Did not the Lord bring us up from Egypt? But now the Lord hath forsaken us, and delivered us into the hands of the Midianites.

And the Lord looked upon him, and said, Go in this thy might, and thou shalt save Israel from the hand of the Midianites: have not I sent thee?

And he said unto him, Oh my Lord, wherewith shall I save Israel? Behold, my family is poor in Manasseh, and I am the least in the father's house."

– *Judges 6:12-15*

Gideon was conditioned by a past life experience of repeated disappointment.

Disappointments are a part of life. There are always going to be things that happen in our lives that we didn't plan for. But these situations don't have to be what mold our identity and determine our destiny. There is a difference between someone who has gone through repeated situations and says, "I'm such a failure, I can't ever make it," and someone who says, "I have failed a few times, but I'm not a failure. I'm on my way to victory!" Failures don't make you a failure. Don't personalize your failure. Learn from it. Don't make excuses for your failures. There is nobody alive that has not done something they wished they'd never done, or tried something and failed, or had a negative situation happen that they did not plan for. Don't fear failure. Some people spend more time fearing fear, fearing what could happen, rather than stepping out and believing that something good could happen. So never allow disappointments to mold your identity because it's not who you are. Every great success in life is always preceded by disappointments that outnumber the success.

Disappointments happen in life, but it doesn't have to mold your identity. Use disappointment as a stepping-stone or a learning tool, not a hammer. Always remember that God has given you the ability to choose life and blessing. The incredible thing about this story is that God doesn't use perfect people. He finds those whose minds have been corrupted and walks them through the renewal process. Gideon allowed God to change his mentality and then went on to join with God and deliver the people from the hand of the enemy.

> "I call heaven and earth to record this
> day against you, that I have set before
> you life and death, blessing and curs-
> ing: therefore choose life, that both
> thou and thy seed may live."
> — *Deuteronomy 30:19*

I am showing you how your soul is developed so you can get it renewed and restored. What happens in you determines what happens through you.

> "A good man out of the good treasure of
> the heart bringeth forth good things:
> and an evil man out of the evil treasure
> bringeth forth evil things."
> — *Matthew 12:35*

We need our souls renewed so that our destiny as God's people can be fulfilled. The problem isn't your environment, spouse, or employer; it is how you have allowed those things to mold your soul. Take personal responsibility to allow the Word to renew your mind and you will begin to experience incredible change in the way your life turns out. Gideon wanted to blame everybody else rather than take personal responsibility for the outcome of his life. When you blame the devil for your prob-lem, you empower him in your life. When you say it's your circumstances that hold you back, you give circumstances control over your life and destiny. It wasn't the giants in the land that stopped Israel from taking Canaan – it was their inability to cope with their preprogrammed Egypt mentality. They were their own snare. Don't allow the enemy or your circumstances to rule your life any longer. Let God's Word change the way you see yourself. You are not a failure. You can do all things through Christ who strengthens you. You aren't going under, you are going over. All things are possible to him that believes.

> *When you say it's your circumstances that hold you back, you give circumstances control over your life and destiny.*

PHYSICAL LIMITATIONS

The last tool the enemy uses against your identity is physical limitations. People have a lack of confidence because of a physical limitation. You might stutter. You might not be able to see very well. You might not run very fast or throw a ball very well. You may be too short, too tall, too skinny, too fat. Your ears are too small. Your nose is too big. You are too pretty and people just use you. You are too ugly and nobody uses you. And you begin to think that your identity is in that. You feel that because you can't do what other people can do you are not a very good person. Moses is an example of this when God told Moses He was sending him to deliver the Israelites:

> "And Moses said unto the Lord, O my Lord, I am not eloquent, neither heretofore, nor since thou hast spoken unto thy servant: but I am slow of speech, and of a slow tongue."
> — *Exodus 4:10*

Moses didn't believe he could do it, but God took this stutterer and turned him into one of the greatest deliverers of all time.

We need to be like the bumblebee. Scientifically, it is impossible for the bumblebee to fly. It is aerodynamically impossible! But the problem is, the bumblebee doesn't know that – and he flies! We need to start believing in the person that God made us to be! Stop allowing physical limitations to destroy your identity in Christ. Again, it's all about what you are presently allowing to form the concepts and beliefs of your inner man. When you get your soul renewed to the Word, you will see a miraculous recovery from what has held you back from fulfilling your destiny and being all that God has made you to be.

Don't you see how much God loves you? He

doesn't want you to live under Satan's deception any longer. God has purchased your freedom from insecurity, rejection, inferiority, fear and bondage in the person of Christ. You don't have to live with the guilt of past sins and abuses. Today, you can reclaim your true identity in Christ if you will only believe. You are what God says you are. You can do what God says you can do. You can have what God says you can have. You are the apple of God's eye. You are God's very own work of art in Christ. Believe it, receive it, and act on it.

CHAPTER 3

BEHOLD, ALL THINGS HAVE BECOME NEW

Many people miss the impact of what God did in Christ. It is centered around identity. When you receive the revelation of what God has done for you in Christ, it will settle some issues in your life once and for all.

This is the heart of the Apostle Paul's teaching to the churches. It is the very revelation that God gave to the Apostle. You cannot find this in the Old Testament; it was hidden from them.

> **"Whereof I am made a minister, according to the dispensation of God which is given to me for you, to fulfill the word of God;**
>
> **Even the mystery which hath been hid from ages and from generations, but now is made manifest to his saints."**
>
> *– Colossians 1:25-26*

So many Christians, who love God with all their hearts and who even attend great churches, have not yet entered into the revelation of who they really are in Christ. They still live like they are under the first Adam. They have not shaken the concept, controls, domination, or mentality of the first

Adam. They limp around in it. Many are born again, go to church, love God, and are filled with the Holy Spirit, but the concept of the first Adam still reigns over their minds and hovers over their souls like a dark cloud. We live like people who are still under the old regime. There has been a regime change. Satan's legal power over our lives has been severed. The corrupted condition, due to Adam's fall in the garden, has been legally released from its control over our lives. We must understand the revelation that the person we used to be is gone. The person we now are in Christ is a totally new person that never existed before.

> *The person we now are in Christ is a totally new person that never existed before.*

Paul Harvey related a story of a young man who had purchased a bird from another young man who had held the bird captive in the cage. The owner of the bird would poke sticks at the bird and torment it. Because the other young man felt compassion for the abused bird, he offered to buy it from the oppressor. After a period of unwillingness to sell, the owner finally decided to sell the bird. The new owner, with excitement, opened the cage to let the bird go free, but because it had been used to the cage and the abuse, it refused to fly free.

After a little coaxing, the bird finally flew to freedom.

Many are like this bird. They are so used to abuse and bondage that they don't know they have been purchased by the blood of Christ and that the door to their freedom is wide open. We need a revelation of our legal right to go free from the bondage that has controlled our lives and to begin to fly free and "mount up on wings, as eagles" (Isaiah 40:31).

> **"Therefore if any man be in Christ, he is a new creature: old things are passed away; behold, all things are become new."**
>
> *— II Corinthians 5:17*

Are you in Christ? "Old things have passed away. Behold, all things have become new." The Holy Spirit is saying, Behold! ALL things have become new.

Some hold a view that those who have accepted Christ have a type of duel nature: the old sin nature and the new nature in Christ. An example of this might be a good dog and bad dog fighting against one another. This view attempts to describe the real conflict that goes on inside of our lives, but it is not really scriptural. The Bible says that man is a three-part person: spirit (our nature), soul (mind, will, emotions, personality), and body (five senses, the earth-suit we live in while in this world).

Your spiritual nature was totally recreated when you made Jesus the Lord of your life. By spiritual nature, we were children of wrath when we were spiritually connected to the kingdom of darkness through our connection with the first Adam. But we did not stay spiritually connected to darkness. We were spiritually born anew. There is, though, a definite struggle that goes on inside our lives. Those who have been given a new nature still have inherited a soul that has been corrupted by the fall. Man's soul (mind, will, and emotions) are predisposed toward worldly, fleshly, and demonic ways of thinking. The real conflict in us is between the truth we hear from God's Word and what is presently programmed in our minds. A major clash of concepts happens inside us. The victory comes when we allow our minds to be renewed to the truth of God's Word. An incredible sense of self-worth and peace is released into our lives when the old, Adamic mentality is replaced by the truth of the Word, the mentality of the new creation. The outcome is the fruit of the Spirit. Fruit is the demonstration of truth through our renewed mind.

"And you hath he quickened, who were dead in trespasses and sins;

Wherein in time past ye walked according to the course of this world, according to the prince of the power of the air, the spirit that now worketh in the children of disobedience:

Among whom also we all had our conversation in times past in the lusts of our flesh, fulfilling the desires of the flesh and of the mind; and were by nature the children of wrath, even as others.

But God, who is rich in mercy, for his great love wherewith he loved us,

Even when we were dead in sins, hath quickened us together with Christ, (by grace ye are saved)."

– *Ephesians 2:1-5*

Your sin nature that you once had is gone. That is a fact. The old spiritual condition, which controlled humanity, has been legally done away with, and by Christ, you have received a new nature. If you will grasp this revelation and begin to apply it to your mind, you will literally come out of the "low life" and into the "high life." You will come out of the old way of living and come into the new way of living. When we give in and let the Word win over in our mind, the battle is over.

God does not want us to just live nice little church lives. You ought to go to church services — the Bible says we are not to forsake the assembling of ourselves together – but there are a lot of nice church folks who attend church and hear the Word but never allow the revelation of the new creation to renew their minds. You can tell by the way they think, by the way they talk, by the way they conduct themselves and their relationships, by how they live in their homes and by what they do for God. You can see it all over them that they still have not come out of the old life. Yes, they love God with all their hearts. They love Jesus. They read their Bibles. They pray. But they have not yet stripped off the concepts and the controls of the old order of things. It's like the children of Israel coming out of Egypt: they came out of bondage, but the bondage never came off of them. They came out of Egypt but Egypt was still on them. When it came time for them to go into the promised land, they could not take it because they still thought as slaves. They still saw themselves in bondage. They didn't see themselves as winners. They didn't see themselves as those united with God Himself. They saw themselves as defeated. They saw themselves as grasshoppers. They did not see themselves as having a relationship with God Almighty. This hindered their lives and kept them from going in and possessing the land and being all that God created them to be. When we call ourselves new creations, yet continue to live and talk and act like old creations, we will not be blessed.

"A double minded man is unstable in all his ways."
— James 1:8

When our minds are not focused and settled on the truth of God's Word, we remain carnal, or mentally of the old regime. This unrenewed mentality brings death. No, you don't fall over and die when you think incorrectly, but it opens the door to the realm of death. Depression, anger, resentment, bitterness, insecurity, and low self-worth work their destructiveness on your destiny. Your destiny was to be like your Creator. It's up to you to break through and receive a revelation.

CRY OUT TO GOD
FOR PERSONAL REVELATION

This bondage over people is being broken. God's people are beginning to rise up and possess in their minds who they now are in Christ. Religion has not satisfied their hunger for true significance. People are getting a revelation of God's Word concerning who they are in Christ.

> "But the natural man receiveth not the things of the Spirit of God: for they are foolishness unto him: neither can he know them, because they are spiritually discerned."
>
> — *I Corinthians 2:14*

The Wuest translation says:

> "The natural man cannot understand the things of the spirit because they are investigated on a spiritual plane."

Investigated. These truths must be personally investigated on a spiritual plane. You must ask for the help of the Holy Spirit to reveal to your heart — to your very inner man — the truth of this revelation. Otherwise you will continue to live out your life the way you were trained, the way you were brought up. Your religious indoctrination will rule you. Your worldly concepts will control your life. You will see life through a different set of glasses, and your life will be lived out by the way you have been trained and developed to see yourself. You will, as the song says, "look for love in all the wrong places." It takes a revelation. Some, however, don't even know that this revelation exists.

The Apostle Paul said:

> "But by the grace of God I am what I am."
>
> — *I Corinthians 15:10(a)*

Paul is saying, "By the grace of God, I am what I am. I am what God says I am. No more, no less than what God says I am. I am not what the devil says I am. I am not what my circumstances say I am. I am not even what Mom and Dad told me I am." It doesn't matter what anybody tells you. When you come into Christ, you start a whole new ballgame. You come into a new order of things. You come into a new life. You let go of the old life and take hold of the new.

Paul had this revelation:

> "Though I might also have confidence in the flesh. If any other man thinketh that he hath whereof he might trust in the flesh, I more:

> Circumcised the eighth day, of the stock of Israel, of the tribe of Benjamin, an Hebrew of the Hebrews; as touching the law, a Pharisee;

> Concerning zeal, persecuting the church; touching the righteousness which is in the law, blameless.

> But what things were gain to me, those I counted loss for Christ.

> Yea doubtless, and I count all things but loss for the excellency of the knowledge of Christ Jesus my Lord: for whom

I have suffered the loss of all things, and do count them but dung, that I may win Christ.

And be found in him, not having mine own righteousness, which is of the law, but that which is through the faith of Christ, the righteousness which is of God by faith."

— *Philippians 3:4-9*

Paul counted the things that were in his past "as dung." He threw them aside. He let them go. He was born of the stock of Israel. He was a Pharisee. He was of the tribe of Benjamin. He was everything in the natural that others might want to be. But as far as Paul was concerned, all those things were gone. He counted everything as dung so that he could win Christ.

You have to let some things go. Let go of some things you value. Let go of the negative things people have told you about yourself in the past. Some people value negative things; they hold onto them very tightly. They don't like it, it doesn't bless them, but they value it because they are familiar with it. Until you let it all go and let God renew your mind and bring a revelation of who you are in Christ, you forfeit the abundant life and Satan will dominate your life. As long as you live under the concepts of the first man, Adam, Satan has control over that area of your life.

The devil doesn't have control over the new things in the spirit; he has no legal control over the new-creation person living in the Word. He has control over the Adamic things. When you live under the earth, earthly, you live carnally. You open the door to the enemy, and the enemy can take control over that area of your life. Any area that has not been transformed into the new-creation life, Satan has a hold of, whether it is a thought or an attitude. The devil can take a bad attitude you have and use it against you because it is of the old regime. It's what gives him place in our lives. He has authority over the old man. He has authority over the first man Adam. That's his regime of rule and anything that touches that realm or allows that realm to be a part of your life gives him dominion, whether it is a thought or a concept. If you say, "I'm such a failure," or, "I'm so worthless," the devil will take that and run with it. It is a concept that is not Biblically true under the new order. You are not a poor, unworthy sinner in Christ. You are the righteousness of God in Christ.

> *You are not a poor, unworthy sinner in Christ. You are the righteousness of God in Christ.*

So if you think and confess, "I'm just a poor, unworthy sinner," you give the devil domination over your life in that area. If you say, "I'm so sick and so poor," you have just given the devil dominion over your life. Why? Because any area where you still allow the old man mentality to rule allows the enemy to rule in that area of your life. That's why the enemy doesn't want your mind renewed. As long as you hold onto unforgiveness, inferiority, insecurity or fear, the devil will use that stronghold in your life to hinder your God-given destiny to rule and reign in Christ.

That is why Jesus said in John 14:30, "The prince of this world cometh, and hath nothing in me." There was nothing in Jesus that connected Him to the Adamic realm. There was nothing in Him that was connected to this world. There was nothing — not a thought, not an opinion, not an attitude, not a concept — that gave the devil place.

The devil looked for something. He certainly tried when he tempted Jesus in the wilderness. He attempted to draw Jesus into the earthly arena of pride and lust but failed because Jesus did not think and live in the Adamic realm. When Jesus said, "It is written...," it is because His life and thinking were totally under the authority of the Word of God, not His flesh, not religious opinion or popular opinion. Jesus was totally separated to truth. He knew His Father. He knew who He was. He was totally given over into this realm. Jesus walked in the true new-creation life, separated from this world and its way of thinking. Satan tried and tried, but he had nothing in Him. It was only until Jesus submitted Himself and said,

> "...I lay down my life, that I might take it again.
>
> No man taketh it from me, but I lay it down of myself. I have power to lay it down, and I have power to take it again. This commandment have I received of my Father."
>
> — *John 10:17(b)-18*

Jesus willingly surrendered Himself. That is the only time the devil had control over His life. Jesus willingly became what we were in the first Adam so that the power of Satan could be legally broken over our lives and we legally could come over into the new-creation realm. Jesus' willing sacrifice of Himself, legally undid what the first Adam had brought upon us through his disobedience.

This is a fact spiritually, but it must become a fact mentally, emotionally, and intellectually. It must be a revelation inside of you, birthed by the power of the Holy Spirit. Until it is, you will continue to live out your life in the old realm. You must reckon the old man as dead.

> **"Likewise reckon ye also yourselves to be dead indeed unto sin, but alive unto God through Jesus Christ our Lord."**
>
> *— Romans 6:11*

If you fail to reckon yourself dead to sin you will continue to live in the flesh. You will continue to do the old things you used to do in your home, and the devil will flood in and try to separate, destroy and hurt your family. There is Adamic stuff still going on, but you can put a stop to it by getting a revelation of the new creation and saying, like Paul, "I am what I am by the grace of God." Confess, "I know who I am. I know everything about who I am. I know Who lives in me. I know what I am capable of doing. I know where my destiny lies. I know what kind of inner person I am. I know what kind of spiritual abilities I possess." Refuse to allow unrenewed mental programming to control your life.

If you fail to reckon yourself dead to sin you will continue to live in the flesh.

People struggle along, trying to get over habits, trying to get demonic forces to stop hindering them, but you must get a revelation in your mind before you can break satanic holds in your life. If you don't want flies around, get the sugar off the table. You can't give the devil place in any area of your life. You must allow the revelation of God to separate you in your mind, emotions, and every area of your life — to separate you and get you sanctified and over into the new-creation realm. That's what sanctification is all about: getting you out of the mentality of the old man, the first man Adam, and pulling you over into the realm of the new-creation mentality. You need to get to the place where you are operating totally and completely out of the revelation of who you are as a new man in Christ in a new relationship with God. Jesus said you will know the truth and the truth will make you free. If you are not bearing fruit, it's because you are living under the old regime. You bite, devour, criticize, pout, whine, and lust. Why? Because your mind is dominated by the old life.

Sin is learned independence from God. When you don't have God, you learn to live independently from Him. In order for your needs to be met, you must go someplace outside of God to get them met. So the devil offers things to you while you are growing up. From the day of your natural birth until now, the enemy has desired to draw you into temptation and convince you that by accepting the offer, your need would be met. We often reach out and take his bait, thinking it will fulfill us emotionally, only to find ourselves wrapped up in all kinds of bondages. Then you get saved and filled with the Holy Spirit, but your mind has been trained to live independently from God. So here you are: a new creature in Christ, yet you don't have a full revelation of all you are in Christ, so all the old bondages are still hanging onto you, controlling you, and Satan is getting hold of your life. Why? Because the revelation has to come in and shatter those things until you begin to realize you don't need anything else but Jesus. He meets your every need, emotionally, physically, and spiritually. You begin to realize you don't need all those other things. You begin to find out who you are. You begin to find out that God has things to give you that make those other things seem like chalk compared to His pearls. What you had in Egypt is nothing to be compared to what's in Canaan. What you had in the low life is nothing to be compared to the high life.

> You cannot consistently live in a way that is inconsistent with the way you see yourself.

God wants the church to begin to realize who they are and not forget it. Don't just hear a message and say, "That was a good message — it made me feel good," or, "That was an interesting concept or idea." It has not become a revelation to you until it has become personalized in your life, when you say, "Bless God, this is mine." You must believe it, receive it, talk it, and act on it.

You cannot consistently live in a way that is inconsistent with the way you see yourself. If you continue to have the concepts of the first man, Adam, you will consistently live in a way that lines itself up with the first man Adam. This will, in turn, attract the evil one to come and rob and steal from you in areas of your life because you give him place.

Sometimes it seems as though outward circumstances happen in your life and you have no control over them. But you *do* have the ability to control what goes on in your life. You have been authorized by God to shut the devil off once and for all, to put the devil to flight, and to live in the realm that is separate from the world system. It's like the Bible says when the people came after Jesus to throw Him off a cliff. Jesus passed through the midst of them and they didn't know where He went. He was untouchable. When the devil tries to hang onto you, you can slip out through his hands. You are so full of life that the enemy can't touch you. Situations can't touch you. You are above it. I am not saying you won't ever have circumstances in life that are challenges, but you are above them.

You are the head, not the tail; above only, not beneath. This is the kind of person God made you in Christ. By taking your place in Christ as righteous, loving, and full of faith, you slam the door on the enemy and prevail over his plan.

CHAPTER 4

THE MAKING
OF THE
NEW MAN

There is a freedom in Christ that you can attain and walk in on a daily basis. You can be free from the bondages of sin, the devil, and negative past experiences and live in a realm that is free and untouched from the realm of bondage. The Holy Spirit has come to remove your burdens and destroy your yokes. But we must know who we are if we are going to begin to walk in this dimension of freedom and liberty. We must acquire a new life and a new mentality to experience the land of abundant life.

"But by the grace of God I am what I am."

— I Corinthians 15:10(a)

Paul knew who he was, just like God knows who He is. When He sent Moses to deliver the children of Israel and Moses asked Him what to tell them, God replied, "Tell them I Am that I Am has sent thee." God knows who He is! This is one of the reasons why the devil has absolutely no authority over God. First of all, He is God. If we had a God who was unsure of who He was, the devil would be able to find a place to mess with Him. If we had a God that had a spirit of inferiority, the devil would find a place to get at Him somehow. But God knows who He is. He is not moved by the devil. God knows that He is love personified. God knows He is righteousness personified. That's why the devil can't come to God and say, "You no good thing, you. You always fail. You can't do anything right. If you did things correctly, a third of your angels would not have left in the beginning and the man you created would have served you. What's wrong with you, God?" God has had plenty of opportunities to get an inferiority complex if He was that kind of a creature. God has not lived a life without any problems. He had the first church split. His first created person chose to disobey Him. God has had His problems. But He knows who He is. He doesn't suffer from an identity crisis. He doesn't let the things that happen to Him destroy who He is.

This is why, when we put on the armor of God, we are able to stand against the plan of the enemy to destroy self-esteem and thwart the destiny of God. God dealt with me about this armor issue. He said this was not something He had in a heavenly closet for His people to visualize putting on every day. This is His armor; it is what makes Him impenetrable to the enemy. The Lord spoke to my heart and said He wanted His people to put on, in their inner man, the stuff that He was made of:

righteousness, truth, peace, etc. This is just another way of saying, "Put on the new man." When you do, your life will be impenetrable. The enemy's attacks and assignments will fail because of what you have become inside through the Word. Once God's armor is appropriated inside, the enemy's attempts to rule you with inferiority will be over because you will know you are the righteousness of God in Christ. New creation realities fortify your inner man and thwart the plan of the enemy to destroy God's plan for your life.

We allow situations to go on in our lives that destroy our identity. Because we have sinned, because we have been involved in certain things, we now feel we are stupid, unclean, and not as good as everybody else. But what you have done in your life does not determine who you are. You are who you are by

> *But what you have done in your life does not determine who you are.*

what God has done for you in Christ and what you now allow to mold your identity. Paul said, "I am what I am by the grace of God." By God's grace — by the work of God — that's what I am. And when you begin to find out who that "I am" is, it will put a stop to all the other junk that the devil has been using to influence you. You will begin to walk out of bondage and into freedom. You, like Paul, must identify with the new person God has made you in the person of Christ, accept that, and let go of the destructive concepts that destroy your future.

The identity crisis is that many Christians don't know who they are. If you are going to walk in freedom, you must know who you are. You must spend time discovering the person that you are now in the person of Jesus Christ because you are not the same person you used to be before you made Jesus the Lord of your life. You have become a totally new person in Christ. Now who is that person?

> "For we are the circumcision, which worship God in the spirit, and rejoice in Christ Jesus, and have no confidence in the flesh."
>
> *— Philippians 3:3*

In order to find out who you are, you must go through the Bible and find out who God says you are. The truth of the Word will give you the ability to discard your old identity. God has created you in Christ to be what you are, and you need to find out what that is. It would have been wrong for Adam to walk around barking like a dog after God created him as a human being in His image and His likeness. There are many people living in ways that God never said they were to live. We are not even aware that some aspects of our lifestyles are contrary to how we were created to live. We just go on, day after day, thinking that everything is fine. But a certain concept, a certain mindset, a certain way of thinking or looking at things, the way you feel about yourself, the way you deal in your relationships with people, are not ways God intends for you to live. How you deal with your relationship to God may not even be based on the Word of God and could be robbing you of true freedom in the person of Jesus Christ. God has set you free completely and released you into a new way of living that is absolutely incredible. Because God sent His Son to earth, something supernatural happened that changed the course of history and the condition of humanity for eternity. To understand it and to receive it will restore you to your true identity and significance.

THE CIRCUMCISION OF GOD IN CHRIST

"And ye are complete in him, which is the head of all principality and power:

In whom also ye are circumcised with the circumcision made without hands, in putting off the body of the sins of the flesh by the circumcision of Christ."

— *Colossians 2:10-11*

"For we are the circumcision, which worship God in the spirit, and rejoice in Christ Jesus, and have no confidence in the flesh."

— *Philippians 3:3*

The Bible declares that we are the circumcision of Christ. What is this circumcision? In the Old Testament, circumcision was the removal of the male foreskin representing the stripping off of the old life and the beginning of a new life of covenant relationship with God. All those desiring covenant with Jehovah were required to be circumcised. In the New Testament, it represents the stripping off of the old condition that ruled the human race in the first Adam and the bringing into existence of a new humanity in covenant relationship with God. This is something God did for us in a spiritual way.

The circumcision of God is a spiritual circumcision, stripping off the old man from humanity and bringing into existence the new man in Christ. It's a spiritual condition. The fallen state of man that gave Satan dominion was stripped off by Jesus 2,000 years ago, but the devil has spent the last 2,000 years working overtime to keep people's minds blinded to this. The god of this world, Satan, blinds the minds of those who still do not believe what the Bible teaches.

"In whom the god of this world hath blinded the minds of them which believe not, lest the light of the glorious gospel of Christ, who is the image of God, should shine unto them."

— II Corinthians 4:4

Satan does not want people to see the truth lest the light of the glorious gospel of Christ, who is the image of God, should shine unto them. When Satan crucified the Lord of Glory, he said, "Ha, ha, we have Him now. We are getting rid of Him." But on the third day, I believe he was saying to himself, "What have I done?"

The devil knows the truth better than Christians do! Because he knows the truth, he becomes the master of deception and keeps people bound. That is why when you know the truth, the truth will make you free.

"And ye shall know the truth, and the truth shall make you free."

— John 8:32

So once you know the truth about the circumcision and work of Christ, the devil's deception is broken and he loses control. He has already lost control legally; his power over human beings now is to deceive them. His greatest tool against the new-creation person is deception. If he can cloud your mind with bondages such as inferiority and fear, even though you are legally free from him, he will attempt to keep you bound on a day-to-day basis.

This is not a physical, outward circumcision, but a spiritual circumcision that God performed by stripping off the fallen Adamic condition that has ruled the human race. He legally stripped it off of humanity. Jesus' death, burial, and resurrection was the tool God used to strip the old Adamic condition off of humanity and bring to life a new-creation humanity.

> **"Buried with him in baptism, wherein also ye are risen with him through the faith of the operation of God, who hath raised him from the dead."**
>
> *— Colossians 2:12*

What God did in Christ through His death, burial, and resurrection was His work of circumcision. It took place from the crucifixion to the seating of Christ at God's right hand. This was the work of circumcision that God did in the spiritual realm. Most people see only the physical side when they look at Jesus on the cross — the suffering Messiah, the blood, the hole in His side. Most of the teaching on the crucifixion deals only with the physical sufferings of Jesus. Very few actually go deeper, behind the veil, to see what was really taking place. Something very powerful was going on in the spirit realm. Jesus not only suffered in the flesh but He suffered in the spirit. He took upon Himself the fallen condition of humanity. He had to become what we were in order to rescue us from what we were.

To understand the spiritual circumcision, we need to know what was stripped off. How can you put off the old man if you don't know what the old man is? When God told Abraham that he needed to circumcise his foreskin, he knew what to circumcise. He understood what that was. Every male at a certain age would also be circumcised if they wanted to enter into covenant with God. Now when God declares that you are the circumcised of the Lord, it represents something God legally stripped off of the human race in the person of His Son. You must know what that was so you can appropriate it by faith in a vital way for your personal life.

When you understand the circumcising work of God in Christ you will have the tools to oppose the carnal realm. Knowing the completed work of spiritual circumcision will give your faith something to work with and the power to then dethrone old strongholds by renewing your mind with truth. You can go from the defeated life into the throne room life. It will take you out of bondage and bring you into victory.

To see the old Adamic man as alive or resurrected gives unrenewed mindsets authority to continue to rule your life.

The legal process took place 2,000 years ago. It is already yours. The Bible says, in Ephesians 1:3, that we have been blessed with all spiritual blessings in heavenly places in Christ. God through Christ did this for you 2,000 years ago. He took the old Adamic nature and stripped it off of the human race. It's gone, it's dead, and it no longer has power and authority over the human race. When faced with temptation, I have heard people say, "The old man wants to resurrect itself." But it can't be resurrected — it's dead, it's stripped off. Jesus killed it. Deception is operating in their minds. The old man cannot resurrect in you! The old man was crucified. If you do not see the old man crucified, the only one suffering is you. To see the old Adamic man as alive or resurrected gives unrenewed mindsets authority to continue to rule your life. Colossians 3:3 says you are dead (the old man) and your life (the new man) is hid "with Christ" in God. So the old man cannot be resurrected in you. You are simply continuing to allow unrenewed Adamic mindsets to suppress your new life in Christ. You have not allowed your mind to be renewed to the truth that the old man is actually dead and that you are now a new creation in Christ. We are controlled by carnality and bondage and waste our destiny when we do not appropriate the truth and allow our minds to be renewed to it.

It is up to humanity to appropriate that realm of victory through faith. When you, by faith, make Jesus Christ the Lord of your life, spiritually that old Adamic condition is immediately stripped off of your spirit. You are no longer an old man; you are a new man in Christ. But your mind, will, and emotions are still dominated by the old Adamic ways. And the way to get that stripped off of your soul is to understand the process of circumcision and apply it to your life, to your soul realm, by faith.

Everyone wants resurrection life. Everyone wants victory over the devil. Everyone wants to walk in prosperity — financially, spiritually, and mentally. But are we willing to do what is necessary to get that freedom? There is no resurrection without first a crucifixion, death, and burial. Jesus didn't go straight to the resurrection. There is a process that Jesus had to go through in order to give us what we have. That process brought legal freedom, and the same process through faith appropriates freedom in your life, thus making it a vital reality in you. Jesus' work in redemption was God's means of stripping off of the human race the condition that destroyed true identity and tied us to a fallen race. Our understanding of God's work in Christ and personal appropriation of it by faith restores true identity in us. When we appropriate the finished work of circumcision by faith, our souls are renewed. Old strongholds are dethroned, and new-creation mindsets are established. This appropriation brings your soul into the same experience that your spirit received at the new birth.

DEATH TO THE OLD — LIFE TO THE NEW

The first thing you must understand and appropriate: YOU ARE CRUCIFIED WITH CHRIST.

> "I am crucified with Christ: nevertheless I live; yet not I, but Christ liveth in me: and the life which I now live in the flesh I live by the faith of the Son of God, who loved me, and gave himself for me."
>
> — *Galatians 2:20*

Paul said, "I am crucified." Remember that Paul said, "I am what I am by the grace of God." He is making what Jesus did here a personal thing. Paul understood the power of substitution. Jesus, as a substitute, took our place as the old Adam, the old man. That is what Jesus was on the cross — He became the old man. Jesus, by way of substitution, became all that we were in Adam on the cross of Calvary. Paul is saying something here that makes it applicable to his everyday life. He didn't say, "Jesus was crucified." He said, "I am crucified with Christ." I, the old man of the Adamic race, with his old insecurities, sins, inferiorities, thinking, and all his other ways, was crucified with Christ. This is something that every human being must do in a personal way. Crucifixion is the supreme decision to commit something to death.

> **"And he went a little farther, and fell on his face, and prayed, saying, O my Father, if it be possible, let this cup pass from me: nevertheless not as I will, but as thou wilt."**
>
> *— Matthew 26:39*

Jesus made the supreme decision to bring something to death. He knew He would take upon Himself all of fallen humanity, and He made the supreme decision to take that thing and commit it to crucifixion. He laid His life down. Nobody forced Him to do it against His will. He said, "I lay my life down. I make the supreme decision to commit all that humanity is in Adam to die." To appropriate this part of the process you must be willing to commit to crucifying those things in your life that you have become accustomed to. Your feelings of insecurity, inferiority, lust, fears, etc., will not want to go to the cross. By faith, you must make the supreme choice to commit these Adamic mindsets to the cross. Look at what Paul said:

> "Knowing this, that our old man is crucified with him, that the body of sin might be destroyed, that henceforth we should not serve sin."
>
> — *Romans 6:6*

Know this. Get a revelation of this. Know that your old man — everything you are under the Adamic condition — was crucified. So why in the world would you allow this to continue to go on? It has already been legally stripped off of you spiritually. He said, "Know this. Get a revelation of this. Get this thing working in your life." Paul had received a revelation of Jesus' substitution and he identified with it in his own life in a personal way. Crucifixion is a choice that we make to commit the old man and all of his intricacies to death. This choice is an act of faith that we make in reckoning the old man as dead.

> "Likewise reckon ye also yourselves to

be dead indeed unto sin, but alive unto God through Jesus Christ our Lord."

— *Romans 6:11*

You will never walk in resurrection life unless you come to a place where you recognize Adamic areas of your life and make the supreme decision to commit them to death. If you don't, it will continue to live on in your life even though you are a new creation. It will allow satanic dominion to rule in that area of your soul, and you will live in bondage as a Christian.

"For to be carnally minded is death; but to be spiritually minded is life and peace."

— *Romans 8:6*

There are two major areas that must be crucified: First, you must crucify your relationship to the old-man existence — everything that pertains to self-will, independence and rebellion. You must see it as crucified. You must not allow it to continue to live on in your life. Why allow something under the old regime to control your life when you could be experiencing freedom, victory, liberty, and prosperity living under the new regime? It will continue to go on only if you allow it to go on. You must make the supreme decision to say, "Everything that the old man is, I commit to crucifixion." There must be a decision of soul to say, "This thing is not a part of who I am; therefore, I commit you to the cross of Calvary. You were crucified with Christ." You make a decision to crucify your relationship to the person outside of Christ in all of his fear, greed, pride, strife, unforgiveness, inferiority, and insecurity. Worldly things keep us from operating in God's supernatural lifestyle.

The second area that must be crucified is your relationship with satanic dominion: sin, sickness, disease, and poverty. This relationship has been crucified with Christ and no longer has the legal right to rule your life. We allow satanic dominion to continue to reign over us when we talk defeat, failure, sickness, weakness, bondage, and depression. When you talk this way, you still see yourself as sick, poverty-stricken and weak. Why do we continue to talk it if we truly don't believe that's what we are? Sickness, disease, and poverty were placed upon the person of Jesus Christ at the crucifixion. They were nailed to the cross of Calvary but your sickness-thinking, poverty-thinking, weak-thinking mind is holding you in bondage. You need to rise up in the name of Jesus and declare that those things were crucified with Christ and begin living in the new-creation realm. Deception is what gives the devil place. When you say, "I'm sick," you are telling the devil that you don't believe that you are free from disease. You have authorized him by virtue of what you have said with your mouth and by virtue of what you still allow to live on in your own personal life. Your new identity gives you connection to the healer, provider, deliverer, etc. We are righteous, blessed, healthy, and prosperous because of who we are now in Christ. The old sinful, sick, defeated person you used to be in Adam was crucified. Now take your faith and appropriate that crucifixion by committing those Adamic areas of your life to the cross. Who you are now, in Christ, is your inheritance. Let the old ways be crucified and get on to the new life. Use your faith and let your mind be renewed.

MAKE IT A DEAD ISSUE

The second thing you must understand and appropriate: YOU ARE DEAD WITH CHRIST.

> **"Now if we be dead with Christ, we believe that we shall also live with him."**
> — *Romans 6:8*

Notice that there is no life without death. Old things must die in order for the new things to live. Not only am I crucified with Christ, but I am also dead with Christ. Everything in this Adamic realm that controlled your life spiritually, mentally, emotionally, was crucified in the person of Jesus and died in Christ. It was accomplished 2,000 years ago. And if the old man, the old realm, is still living in you today, you must be honest with yourself. You must take personal responsibility to put off the old man and put on the new man. We put off by faith what Jesus put off 2,000 years ago, and we put on by faith what Jesus put on for us 2,000 years ago.

Death is the inevitable consequence of crucifixion. Things don't die unless you make the supreme decision to put them on the cross. You must commit all that is Adamic in your life to death. You must say, "This man is not going to be sick any more. I'm taking that sick mentality and it's going on the cross." And when you go through this process you won't say, "Well, I was doing all right for awhile, but now I think I'm sick." No, when you put something to death, it becomes a dead issue. And when it's a dead issue, *it's a dead issue!* The devil can't raise something up that is a dead issue, and you won't be able to either, if it's truly a dead issue in your mind. The reason we sometimes think the old man is raising up again and trying to come to life again is because we haven't actually crucified

> *You must take personal responsibility to put off the old man and put on the new man.*

it. We haven't allowed it to die in us. We haven't allowed it to become a *dead issue* inside of us. We see ourselves defeated, sick, poor, and unrighteous. It is not registered in our soul realm as a crucified and dead thing.

Death marks the end of a relationship to a thing. Your relationship to the old man and his deeds must become a dead issue in your life in order for you to begin to move into a new realm and begin to experience what God has for you. Many are not experiencing resurrection life because they have not reckoned the old-man mentality, and his deeds, dead by faith. There is no resurrection from heaven until you commit things that are in the old Adamic realm to crucifixion and death. New-creation realities are raised up in you when the old Adamic ways of thinking are reckoned dead. We hold on too tightly to that which we are familiar with instead of crucifying it and allowing it to die so that we can reach out and take hold of the new supernatural way of living in the person of Jesus Christ. In Christ's death, the Adamic condition was abolished, and it is now a dead issue with God. Satan cannot bring it up because it is a dead issue. He can't go to God and bring it up because the devil knows it's a dead issue. He can only go to you.

"If ye then be risen with Christ, seek those things which are above, where

Christ sitteth on the right hand of God.

Set your affection on things above, not on things on the earth.

For ye are dead, and your life is hid with Christ in God."

— *Colossians 3:1-3*

The old man is dead, and your life is now hid with Christ in God. Commit that inferior, bitter, sick, unforgiving, defeated person to death and allow God to resurrect the new mentality in you. The problem has been that we have tried to pick fruit instead of destroying the tree. According to Galatians 5, the works of the flesh are adultery, fornication, uncleanness, lasciviousness, idolatry, witchcraft, hatred, variance, emulations, wrath, strife, sedition, heresy, envy, murder, drunkenness, reveling, etc. This is the fruit of the old man under the first Adam. Unrenewed souls enable this type of fruit to continue manifesting itself in one's life even as a Christian. But the fruit of the spirit is love, joy, peace, longsuffering, gentleness, goodness, faith, meekness, and temperance. This is the fruit of the new man in Christ whose soul has been renewed. What many have been doing is emphasizing the fruit. When an old Adamic thing that controls your soul realm crops up, you say, "I bind you, I bind you, I'm not going to do that," and it continues to live in your life. You must take the tree and kill it. The old tree must die before new fruit of the new life can come to pass. If all you do is pick fruit, e.g., "Anger, I bind you," "Envy, I bind you," the tree is still living and bad fruit will pop out in another realm. There is obviously something still living in you that produces bad fruit. In Luke 3:9, Jesus said that every tree that does not bear good fruit is cut down and thrown into the fire. He was saying, "I'm going to kill the tree that has been bringing the old Adamic fruit. I'm going to strip it off of you and then you are going to get a revelation of it and apply faith to what I did 2,000 years ago. You need to say, "That old tree is dead and I'm a new tree — new in Christ — and I am bringing forth fruit unto God." This is an absolute fact. Believe it about yourself!

> **"Likewise reckon ye also yourselves to be dead indeed unto sin, but alive unto God through Jesus Christ our Lord."**
> — *Romans 6:11*

You must reckon this done by faith. Reckon yourselves "dead indeed unto sin." Paul did not say to go around saying, "I'm just a poor unworthy sinner." He said to reckon yourself dead to sin, reckon sin to be a dead issue in your life. It is not humility to say you are an unworthy sinner; it is ignorance of who you are in Christ. You are not a sin-ridden being anymore. You have a new nature. You are an off-spring of God Almighty. His Spirit is in your spirit. His life is in your spirit. His nature is in your spirit. You have divine union with God. You are a God-kind of being. You are a new species of being; that old thing died. You have been created in righteous-ness and true holiness. You are the righteousness of God in Christ. Let the soul catch up to this. Start applying the truth of crucifixion and death. See yourself dead to satanic domination. Hebrews 2:14 says that Jesus partook of flesh and blood that through death He might destroy him who had the power of death, that is, the devil. Your connection with the devil has been severed. Satan no longer has authority over your life. He is not your lord.

REST IN PEACE

The third thing you must understand and appro-priate: YOU ARE BURIED WITH CHRIST.

> **"Therefore we are buried with him by baptism into death: that like as Christ was raised up from the dead by the glory of the Father, even so we also should walk in newness of life."**
>
> *— Romans 6:4*

First, you accept that the old man is crucified.

You believe it. It becomes a reality inside of you that the old man is crucified. You make it a dead issue. And then you bury it. Burial is the laying to rest of something once and for all. You put your RIP -- Rest In Peace -- over that thing. The Son of God buried the old man in the lower parts of the earth. He never came back to life. Jesus became the firstborn from the dead. He was the firstborn of a new creation. That person He was on the cross, the Adamic man, was buried and stayed buried. Jesus didn't raise up an old sinful man. He didn't raise up an unrighteous person. He arose the firstborn of a new race of beings. When you put that thing to rest, it won't come back to life. Jesus crucified it. The old man and his condition are gone. Let him rest in peace and get on with your new-creation life. God's freedom is just waiting to be appropriated. Many of you are allowing past situations, hurts and rejections to live on in your life. It's time to lay them to rest and get on in your freedom in Christ.

THE RESURRECTION OF THE NEW SELF

The fourth thing you must understand and appropriate: YOU ARE RAISED WITH CHRIST.

"That I may know him, and the power of his resurrection..."

— Philippians 3:10(a)

Notice that Paul said "power of His resurrection." Some people say, "It was all done at the cross." No, resurrection could have happened without the cross, but it wasn't all done at the cross. Even in the Old Testament, when the lamb was slain, that was not all there was to it. The blood had to be taken into the Holy of Holies. Redemption didn't stop at the cross. Jesus had to take the blood into the heavenly Holy of Holies before His work was complete. It is all inclusive — it is Jesus' death, burial, resurrection, and ascension that totally redeems humanity. If it had all been done at the cross, then Paul missed it because Paul said:

> "But if there be no resurrection of the dead, then is Christ not risen:
>
> And if Christ be not risen, then is our preaching vain, and your faith is also vain.
>
> Yea, and we are found false witnesses of God; because we have testified of God that he raised up Christ: whom he raised not up, if so be that the dead rise not.
>
> For if the dead rise not, then is not Christ raised:
>
> And if Christ be not raised, your faith is

vain; ye are yet in your sins."

— I Corinthians 15:13-17

If Christ was not raised up, you are still in your sins. Something powerful and supernatural and dynamic and glorious beyond the human imagination took place at the resurrection. Paul desired to experience the power of His resurrection. Why do we want to know the power of His resurrection? Because it has everything to do with our new condition. Resurrection replaces the old with a new. God doesn't just remove a fallen condition; He raises up and replaces the condition with a new creation.

God wants your understanding to be enlightened as to what He has done for you in the person of Jesus Christ in this work of circumcision. He wants your eyes to be opened concerning the putting off of the old man and the bringing in of the new man. When Adam and Eve sinned, their eyes were opened — they got a revelation. But it was a revelation of a fallen condition, a godless condition. God is now waiting on the new-creation people to get a revelation, to get their eyes opened to the new-creation reality. Many still focus only on the Adamic condition and miss the new-creation condition.

"Therefore if any man be in Christ, he is

a new creature: old things are passed away; behold, all things are become new."

— *II Corinthians 5:17*

Paul, by revelation, said:

"That the God of our Lord Jesus Christ, the Father of glory, may give unto you the spirit of wisdom and revelation in the knowledge of him:

The eyes of your understanding being enlightened; that ye may know what is the hope of his calling, and what the riches of the glory of his inheritance in the saints,

And what is the exceeding greatness of his power to us-ward who believe, according to the working of his mighty power,

Which he wrought in Christ, when he raised him from the dead, and set him at his own right hand in the heavenly places."

— *Ephesians 1:17-20*

Something very powerful took place at the resurrection. The Word says that the exceeding greatness of God's power was released to us. This word "power" is the Greek word "dunamis" or dynamite. It tells us that this dynamite was made possible because of the working of His mighty power in raising Jesus from the dead. This latter word for power is the Greek word "kratos." It means God's might. It comes from the root "kra," meaning the workings of a creator — the creative power of God. Paul was revealing to humanity that the exceeding greatness of God's dynamite was released to us in the work of His creative power when He raised Christ from the dead. Why? Because when He raised Christ from the dead He raised you from the dead. God's creative power raised to life a fallen humanity in the person of Christ. All of the blessings of heaven were released and restored back to this new humanity at the resurrection. Jesus was put to death for your transgressions and He was raised again for your justification. When Jesus arose, you arose. When Jesus was on the cross, you were on the cross. And when He walked over to the devil and said, "I will take those keys now," that was you taking the keys. When the devil looked into Jesus' eyes he saw you saying, "Gimme them keys, Jack, you are through!" Why? Because through substitution, Jesus was taking our place. The devil knew he had been stripped of his power. He knew he no longer had the ability to rule. The Bible says that had the devil known this he never would have crucified the Lord of Glory. Had he known what he was doing he never would have planted the Son of God. This is the whole meaning of substitution. Jesus became what we were so that we could become what He is. We were cruci-fied with Him, died with Him, were buried with Him, and are now raised with Him.

> *Jesus became what we were so we could become what He now is.*

Now resurrection is an overall term for the rais-ing up of Christ, but there are two parts to it: the physical resurrection and the spiritual resurrec-tion. Jesus was not only raised physically but spir-itually. Jesus, on the cross, took the Adamic condi-tion of the human race and crucified, put to death and buried the old man. But on the third day God raised up a new humanity free from spiritual death, disease, poverty and satanic domination.

Jesus became what we were so we could become what He now is.

"And you hath he quickened, who were dead in trespasses and sins;

Wherein in time past ye walked accord-ing to the course of this world, accord-ing to the prince of the power of the air, the spirit that now worketh in the children of disobedience:

Among whom also we all had our conversation in times past in the lusts of our flesh, fulfilling the desires of the flesh and of the mind; and were by nature the children of wrath, even as others.

But God, who is rich in mercy, for his great love wherewith he loved us,

Even when we were dead in sins, hath quickened us together with Christ, (by grace ye are saved;)

And hath raised us up together, and made us sit together in heavenly places in Christ Jesus."

— Ephesians 2:1-6

RESURRECTION BRINGS NEW SPIRITUAL LIFE

The first thing resurrection brings is new spiritual life.

"And from Jesus Christ, who is the faithful witness, and the first begotten of the dead."

— Revelation 1:5(a)

Jesus is not the first begotten of the physical dead. He raised Lazarus while He was here on earth. Elijah saw people raised from the dead. Jesus was not the first to come out of physical death, but He was the first to be born out of spiritual death into new-creation life. The Word says in Ephesians 2:5 that when we were "dead in trespasses and sins" (spiritual death, not physical) that we were made alive together with Christ. We were not made physically alive with Christ, but rather we were made spiritually alive with Christ. In Christ we are no longer bound by spiritual death but we have been made spiritually alive through what Christ brought to us in His resurrection. There was a begetting, a birthing, in the resurrection. The One who was dead has now become alive. He went to the lower parts of the earth, to hell, but God's spirit entered into Him and He became the firstborn among many brethren. He stepped out of the womb in the lower parts of the earth as the first of the new creation. He was the first to come out of death into life, from the fallen Adamic condition into the new-creation condition. The resurrection was the bringing to life of a dead humanity, a satanically dominated humanity. It, in Christ being made alive, was the bringing about of a new nature. You and I were made alive in Christ. A whole new humanity was birthed in the resurrection of Christ. This is the new creation of God for the human race in Christ.

The devil looked on and saw all of this taking place and thought, "Oh, my! The entire human race right there in the person of Christ was made alive." Satan saw all of his dominion fall off because death and darkness no longer had control over the human race. It fell off in Christ. And on the day of Pentecost the devil must have really freaked out! After Peter stood up and started to preach, a few thousand in the same mold as Jesus came up. He saw them walking out from under his dominion. They were being healed, blessed and delivered. He had to round up his demons and try to stop it by polluting their minds and telling them it wasn't so, telling them they were just weak, poor, unworthy sinners saved by grace, getting them to talk defeat, sickness and disease. The devil knows more about this stuff than the Church! It's the best kept secret there is!

> *Satan saw all of his dominion fall off because death and darkness no longer had control over the human race.*

RESURRECTION BRINGS VICTORY

Secondly, resurrection brings victory and release from satanic domination. Jesus put off from him the principalities and powers.

> "And having spoiled principalities
> and powers, he made a shew of them
> openly, triumphing over them in it."
>
> — *Colossians 2:15*

This happened when Jesus was made alive. The word for "put off" in the Greek means: to strip off, to put off, to literally spoil. It was in the lower parts of the earth that Jesus spoiled principalities and powers.

> "And what is the exceeding greatness of
> his power to us-ward who believe,
> according to the working of his mighty
> power,
>
> Which he wrought in Christ, when he
> raised him from the dead, and set him
> at his own right hand in the heavenly
> places,
>
> Far above all principality, and power,
> and might, and dominion, and every
> name that is named, not only in this
> world, but also in that which is to
> come."
>
> — *Ephesians 1:19-21*

God raised Jesus up far above all the principalities and powers, and He raised you up with Him.

Your position is above every demonic force, whether it is a principality, a power or a ruler of the darkness. And it's all because of what He did in making Jesus alive in hell.

> "And hath put all things under his feet, and gave him to be the head over all things to the church.
>
> Which is his body, the fullness of him that filleth all in all."
> — *Ephesians 1:22-23*

The body is connected to the head. We are the body and Jesus is the head. The Bible says that all things are placed under His feet, and all things are placed under our feet because we are the body of Christ. He is the head. We are His body.

> "For we are his workmanship, created in Christ Jesus unto good works, which God hath before ordained that we should walk in them."
> — *Ephesians 2:10*

You are God's very own work of art created in Christ. You are God's masterpiece. This work of art took place when God raised Jesus from the dead. He created a whole new race of being. His creative power brought into existence a redeemed race. What a stroke of genius! When Jesus came alive and a new creation was birthed, He put off from Him principalities and powers. At that very moment Satan lost his rule. New life broke the hold of death over humanity. Satan's nature no longer had legal claim over our lives. This was the purpose for which the very Son of God was manifest — that He might destroy the works of the devil.

> **"Forasmuch then as the children are partakers of flesh and blood, he also himself likewise took part of the same; that through death he might destroy him that had the power of death, that is, the devil."**
>
> *— Hebrews 2:14*

The word "destroy" means to dethrone. Jesus dethroned the Lord of Death. He dethroned him off of your life. Whatever rule Satan had in your life has been broken off by Christ. Sin, sickness, disease, poverty, carnality, etc., have lost their legal control in Christ if you will understand and identify with it. Satan's dominion has been stripped off of you. His hold is abolished, because the old Adamic man that gave him dominion was crucified, destroyed and buried. Jesus raised up a new man in Himself and Satan has no connection to him.

This is the triumphant new creation. God raised

us out of the realm of death and darkness. This is the emergence of a whole new creation vested with heavenly favor and awesome power. This is the new creation — coming out of death, hell and the grave. This is the new creation — being raised up out of the realm of darkness not to be held by its control. The major portion of victory took place right in the very lower regions of hell. It doesn't matter how dark things look for you. No matter how bad things look, if you feel like you are in the lower part of hell, no matter how sinful things have been, you can come out of it. God's mercy has been extended to the worst of sinners. God's mercy has been extended to the sickest person. God's love and mercy have been extended to the most depraved human being. No matter where you are, no matter what you've been through, no matter what is going on right now in your life, God loves you and He has extended forgiveness to you in the person of Jesus Christ. He is not looking at your failures; He is looking at His Son's victory and saying, "All that are sinful, defeated, brokenhearted, in bondage to the enemy — a new thing has happened. You have conquered with Christ. You are made alive with Christ. You have been raised with Christ." It's time to let the old die and be buried. It's time to identify with the new life in Christ.

SEATED WITH CHRIST

The last thing you must understand and appropriate: YOU ARE SEATED WITH CHRIST.

> **Seating is a position of authority. You have positional authority at the right hand of God Almighty.**

> **"And hath raised us up together, and made us sit together in heavenly places in Christ Jesus."**

> *— Ephesians 2:6*

Not only did He raise you up out of miry clay and set you on a solid rock, but He also seated you in heavenly places. The Bible says we were raised together with Him and He made us to sit with him in heavenly places. He made you sit. He gave you authority. He said you are now authorized to rule.

Jesus raised up a new man in Himself and Satan has no connection to him.

The Bible says that Jesus is sitting, expecting until His enemies are made His footstool. What is He waiting on? He is waiting for the Church to rise up in Jesus' name. He is waiting for the Church to find their place and begin to exercise dominion over the defeated foe. Take your rightful place. Rise up. You are no longer dead in sin — you are alive. You are righteous. Death, hell, and the grave can no longer keep you bound; you have been raised up out of it and you are now seated and authorized. Psalm 8 says that in the beginning God gave His human race dominion over all the works of His hands — all things were under his feet. Death made use of the one individual, Adam, to seize man's ability to reign in life. Adam's disobedience disconnected His spirit from God, the source of life and the ability to reign. Adam's spirit, severed from God, connected humanity to a nature that reduced him to slavery and brought him under the dominion of his new lord, Satan. In Adam, all things were swept out from under the feet of humanity, but in Christ all things were brought back under our feet. In Christ we now reign in life through one Jesus Christ.

> "For if, through the transgression of the one individual, Death made use of the one individual to seize the sovereignty, all the more shall those who receive God's overflowing grace and gift of righteousness reign as kings in Life through the one individual, Jesus Christ."
>
> *— Romans 5:17, Weymouth*

God made you to sit with Christ at His right

hand. You have been given incredible authority from God. His purpose is for you to reign in life. You are no longer the dominated, you are the dominator. You are the head, not the tail. Above only and not beneath. This is what your new relationship with God has made you. Put off the old man and put on the new. It's time to reign. It's time to exercise dominion for the Kingdom of God. You have been delivered out of the dominion of darkness.

> **"Who hath delivered us from the power of darkness, and hath translated us into the kingdom of his dear Son."**
> — *Colossians 1:13*

You are no longer under satanic dominion. You have authority in Christ over sin, disease, bondage, fear, and all the other works of the devil. Take your place and put the devil in his. Be renewed in the spirit of your mind. Put on a dominator's thinking, not a dominated thinking. Let your mind be renewed to your new position in Christ and rule now "in the midst of thine enemies."

CHAPTER 5

STEPS TO THE NEW YOU

The Bible says that you are wonderfully made! God didn't make a mistake when He made you.

> "And God saw everything that he had made, and, behold, it was very good."
>
> *— Genesis 1:31(a)*

The Bible says that you are God's workmanship, created in Christ.

> "For we are his workmanship, created in Christ Jesus unto good works, which God hath before ordained that we should walk in them."
>
> *— Ephesians 2:10*

You are God's work of art. There are three major steps to the new you.

SEE YOURSELF AS GOD SEES YOU

The first step to the new you is to start seeing yourself as God sees you. This is the true picture from God of who you really are now as a believer. The new you is the new person in Christ. The person you used to be under the first Adam is gone.

You were born into this world in the family of the first Adam. You were separated from God and under the power and control of the evil one. When you were born again, you were born into the family of the last Adam, Jesus Christ, and have been brought out of darkness and into His marvelous light.

> "Giving thanks unto the Father, which hath made us meet to be partakers of the inheritance of the saints in light:
>
> Who hath delivered us from the power of darkness, and hath translated us into the kingdom of his dear Son."
>
> — *Colossians 1:12-13*

You have a new life in Christ. The moment you made Jesus the Lord of your life you were brought out of darkness and you came into light. Church does not save you. Being born again through Christ does. When you are born again, there is a spiritual change; there is a re-creation of the human spirit. A new person is birthed into existence.

The new you is the new person in Christ.

If you are living your life through an Egypt mentality you will never experience the fullness of God for your life; your destiny as a new creation will slip away from you.

> **"For if any be a hearer of the word, and not a doer, he is like unto a man beholding his natural face in a glass:**
>
> **For he beholdeth himself, and goeth his way, and straightway forgetteth what manner of man he was."**
>
> *— James 1:23-24*

Many, many Christians are forgetful hearers. It is not easy to break old mindsets that have been operating in our lives for years and years, but in order to enjoy God's fullness of life and joy, they must be broken. Freedom is better than fear. Many people have been hurt, bruised and kicked around, leading to feelings of rejection. They feel like nobody loves them. But God says you have been released from that. You don't have to live like that any longer.

God is your Father and you are His offspring. The One who spoke everything into existence is in truth your Daddy God. Your Daddy. Maybe your parents spoke a lot of things over you, or maybe someone abused you. But it's time to let your Daddy God influence you. It's time to take His idea of your life. He says that when you are a hearer of the Word and not a doer, you are like a person who looks into a mirror but forgets what manner of man he is.

The Message translation says:

> "Those that hear and don't act are like those who glance in the mirror, walk away and two minutes later have no idea who they are or what they look like."
>
> — *James 1:23-24*

If you look in a mirror, what do you see? Most people will say, "Brown hair," or, "Red tie." But how many actually look into the spirit and say, "Look at that son of God." When I look into the mirror I say to myself, "My goodness, look at that — the righteousness of God in Christ," or, "A new species."

When Jesus rose again from the dead, He created a new humanity. The Bible clearly says you are a son or daughter of God, a new creation, the righteousness of God in Christ Jesus. But you look in the mirror and say, "Pathetic." You may not come right out and say it, but inside you think, "Man, I'm such a failure. I've tried so many things; I can't seem to get anything right." This is because you have the wrong picture of yourself.

My son brought me a picture he had found of me in my old life, in my BC years (Before Christ.) I was in an apartment and my hair was down to the middle of my back and I was holding a fifth of Jack Daniels. That person was the old man in Adam — that's not me today. That old person died 2,000 years ago because Jesus crucified the old man. The old man is gone. I am a new creation in Christ. I now, by faith, accept the fact that God has made me a whole different person inside. I choose to believe that and accept that as my new identity in Christ.

> "Therefore if any man be in Christ, he is a new creature: old things are passed away; behold, all things are become new."
>
> *— II Corinthians 5:17*

I don't want to reinforce an old picture. I don't want to see myself like I used to be. This is not denial. It's receiving truth into my soul so I can be transformed from the pre-programmed way of living under the first Adam life. I want to get a revelation and see myself the way I am now in Christ. You will never rise above what you perceive yourself to be. You will never rise above how you see yourself inwardly. If you see yourself as a drug addict, you will eventually go out and do drugs. Remember, you cannot consistently live in a way that is inconsistent with the way you

You will never rise above how you see yourself inwardly.

see yourself. You need to be honest. How do you really see yourself? Where did that image come from? You must get a revelation when you look in the mirror of God's Word. You must see more than what you used to be. You must begin to see who God has made you to be. You must let go of your old hurts and your old failures and lay hold of your victory in Christ. We need to stop blaming our past and take responsibility for our future. We need to let Jesus be the picture we look at and say, "That's me. I'm in Christ. I'm going to go higher. Life is going to get better from this day on. Why? Because I am more than a conqueror through Him that loved me."

This is not denial. We don't deny the fact that we have missed it, that we do human things, that we do wrong things. I am not talking about being an ostrich and hiding your head in the sand. But when you miss it, you must not allow that to control your identity. You simply allow God's Word to control your identity and grow up. Grow up and be what God has called you to be.

Look into the perfect law of liberty. Look in the mirror of God's Word and don't leave after two minutes and forget what manner of man you are. The Phillips Translation of II Corinthians 3:18 says, "We are transfigured by the Spirit of the Lord in ever-increasing splendor into His own image" as we allow the Word of God to transform our minds.

If the Bible says you are a child of God, then you are a child of God. Spend time in the Word of God and find out what a child of God is. What does it mean when you look in the mirror and say, "There is a temple of the most high God. God no longer dwells in temples made with hands. I have become the temple of the Holy Ghost." What does that mean? It means that the place that God lives is right here. Some people cry out, "Oh, God, I need more power." You don't need more power — you need a revelation of who already lives on the inside of you. You are wall-to-wall God right now. What more do you need? You are the temple of God, and the temple is where God dwells.

"...because greater is he that is in you, than he that is in the world.
— I John 4:4(b)

Instead of saying, "I don't know if I'm going to make it," why not look into the New Testament mirror and start saying, "God lives in me." Instead of saying, "I'm so unclean, so unworthy, God doesn't love me," why not look in the New Testament mirror and say, "I have been washed clean by the blood of Jesus. I am a new creature. I am not an old sinful thing. I have been cleansed and washed. There is no more room for guilt. There is no more room for shame. I have become the righteousness of God in Christ."

"For he hath made him to be sin for us, who knew no sin; that we might be made the righteousness of God in him."

— II Corinthians 5:21

The Bible says you are the righteousness of God in Christ. You were made righteous with God's righteousness; therefore, you are as righteous as God is. You are not who you are because of what you do. You are who you are because of what Jesus has done for you. If you could have produced your salvation there would have been no need for Jesus to come. He doesn't need your help; He needs your cooperation. Many of us have a "Messiah complex" and think, "I've got to do something to get my salvation." No, all you have to do to get salvation is believe on what He did for you; He does the rest. You just continue to believe in who you are. Continue to stand in your righteousness. Continue to stand in your new identity. Continue to walk with God like you believe the Bible is true. Continue to live that life out and you will begin to see your life change. I was taught these things

> *You are who you are because of what Jesus has done for you.*

when I was first born again, and I thank God for it. I didn't have to sit around and say, "I'm just a recovering drug addict." That old man I used to be is dead and gone.

WORK ON A FACELIFT

Second, you must get to work on a personal facelift. Don't just lay down and expect transformation to happen! Transformation is a cooperation. What do you want your life to be like? You must go in and possess the land. What God did for you legally in the work of His Son must be vitally appropriated by you through faith.

> "Speak unto the children of Israel, and say unto them, When ye are passed over Jordan into the land of Canaan;
>
> Then ye shall drive out all the inhabitants of the land from before you, and destroy all their pictures, and destroy all their molten images, and quite pluck down all their high places:
>
> And ye shall dispossess the inhabitants of the land, and dwell therein: for I have given you the land to possess it."
>
> — *Numbers 33:51-53*

The land of Canaan was God's legal inheritance

Invest in yourself by meditating, reading, and memorizing Scripture that establishes your true identity.

that the children of Israel were required to possess as their own. God told the Israelites to drive out all the inhabitants in the land. What are the inhabitants in your land? They are mindsets that have been preprogrammed into our lives. For example, perhaps you feel inferior. Do you get around certain people and feel intimidated? Does somebody say something and you feel inferior? Do you get around a group of people and all of a sudden you feel like you don't want to be there because your hair looks stupid or your nose is too big? All your identity is found in some physical thing. Who do you think you are? Go to work on that thing. When you look in the mirror, the face you see should be the one that God has created you to have. Let the Word of God and the Spirit of God give you a different view of the person you see in the mirror.

You must allow the Word to re-educate your soul. Go to the Word of God and believe, receive, talk and act like what you read is true, because it is. Don't just sit around, hoping that transformation will come. When you start waking up in the morning and saying, "I am a child of God," waking up knowing you are the righteousness of God in

Christ, it will do something in you. A new joy will begin to spring forth in your life. A new energy will begin to come. You will begin to see life from a whole different perspective. You will walk around knowing that Daddy God is your Daddy. You will walk around knowing that somebody bigger than yourself lives inside of you — the one who spoke the worlds into existence resides in you. God is looking for people bold enough to believe the truth.

> **"Know ye not that ye are the temple of God, and that the Spirit of God dwelleth in you?"**
>
> — *I Corinthians 3:16*

If you really believe that God dwells in you, you need to act like it and talk like it. Remember, the greater one is in you. Invest in yourself by meditating, reading, and memorizing Scripture that establishes your true identity. Read the Word of God and search out all the Scriptures that talk about "in Him," "in Whom," and "in Christ." Read books that teach you who you are in Christ. Meditate, meditate, meditate, and assimilate it. It won't happen overnight. You did not get where you are right now overnight. The same way destructive mindsets were established will be the way Biblical ones will be established. We need long-term exposure to a Holy Ghost environment, and we need godly and traumatic experiences with God that stimulate godly perceptions that develop strongholds for God in our lives.

INVOLVE QUALITY PEOPLE

Third, involve quality people in your life. Fear and inferiority are contagious. Don't cut yourself off from loving and caring about people, but realize the effect that certain personal relationships will have upon your life. If a particular person is always negative, decide not to associate with him right now. Associations do influence the way you see yourself. Involve yourself with people that will stretch you to be all you were created to be in Christ. Fight the temptation to hang around those who only reinforce carnal and fleshly living. Remember, beliefs, attitudes, and lifestyles are incredibly contagious. Hang around men and women who will infect your soul with truth, faith and new-creation realities.

Associations do influence the way you see yourself.

Be wise concerning your relationships as you grow in Christ. Evil communication corrupts good behavior. As you grow in Christ, your spirit will begin to be a great blessing and source of support and encouragement for someone seeking after God or desiring spiritual growth as a Christian. Letting quality people into your life will be a great resource for helping you grow in Christ.

HELP SOMEONE ELSE

Fourth, reach out and help someone else get there. If you know someone who is always talking negatively, you don't want to be influenced by him, but you can help him by talking new-creation truths to him. Testify of the goodness of God to him. Speak the Word to him. You don't need to beat him over the head with your Bible, but speak words of life to him, words that will build him up. Help others see their new-found identity in Christ. Hurting people hurt people. Let's introduce them to a new way of life and help them find healing and wholeness. What you make happen for others, God will make happen for you.

Help others see their new-found identity in Christ.

Find an avenue to put your new love-nature, your new joy-nature, into practice. Find somebody to love. Find somebody to bless. Find somebody to lift. Find a new place for this new attitude in Christ to come out on the job and in the family. Look for opportunities to show somebody that there is a God that is alive and He is on the inside of you.

Be what God has called you to be. Believe it in your heart, confess it with your mouth and act like it is so, because it is. Never again settle for anything less about yourself than what God says about you. This new life in Christ cost Jesus His life for you to have. Go ahead and be what God has made you in Christ. It is who you are!

Now, who do you think you are?